ONCE AN ADDICT

ONCE AN ADDICT

The fascinating true story of one man's
escape from the murky drugs underworld

Barry Woodward
with Andrew Chamberlain

Authentic

MILTON KEYNES ● COLORADO SPRINGS ● HYDERABAD

15 14 13 12 11 10 09   13 12 11 10 9 8 7

Reprinted 2007 (2), 2008 (3), 2009

First published 2007 by Authentic Media
9 Holdom Avenue, Bletchley, Milton Keynes, MK1 1QR, UK
1820 Jet Stream Drive , Colorado Springs, CO 80921, USA
OM Authentic Media, Medchal Road, Jeedimetla Village,
Secunderabad 500 055, A.P., India
www.authenticmedia.co.uk
Authentic Media is a division of IBS-STL UK, a company limited by
guarantee (registered charity no. 270162)

British Library Cataloguing in Publication Data
A catalogue record for this book is available from the
British Library

ISBN 978-1-86024-602-9

Cover Design by David Lund Design
Print Management by Adare Carwin
Printed and bound in the UK by J F Print Ltd., Sparkford, Somerset

I dedicate this book to Alan Reeve.
I will never forget how much time and energy you invested in me during the key turning-point in my life.

This is the true story of my life. However, the names of some people and places have been changed or omitted to protect the identities of individuals.

Contents

Acknowledgements

I would like to thank Andrew Chamberlain, my co-writer, for all his hard work and dedication. It's been good to work together with you on the original manuscript. I would also like to thank Malcolm Down at Authentic Media for his commitment to and belief in this book, and a big thanks to all the Authentic team for taking this on. I must also say thanks to my friend and mentor, J.John, for his advice and encouragement during this venture. Last but not least, I would like to thank my wife Tina for all her support and patience during the times when I was totally consumed by this project.

Acknowledgements

Foreword

We are all needy people and we're driven to meet those needs in a variety of ways. We all need to be loved and accepted for who we are and we're all looking for some affirmation in life. For various reasons, people turn to alcohol and drugs to help them with the ups and downs of life. Some people experiment with alcohol and drugs for social reasons; it becomes a means to get rid of inhibitions or to be a part of the crowd. Others turn to chemical substances as a means to cope with or to ease the pain – a pain that can be either physical or emotional. The only problem is the 'high' or relief is only short-lived.

We live in an addicted society. There are more types of addictions than we can imagine. People have found themselves addicted to many conscious and unconscious obsessions: cigarettes, cigars, alcohol, drugs, prescription medications, shopping, work, gambling, anger, rage, gossiping, selfishness, over-eating, under-eating, over-spending, envy, jealousy. Well-meaning people can even find themselves addicted to good things like exercise, or sex which leads into affairs, unhealthy cyber-relationships and pornography.

Sadly, many people are trapped in a lifestyle of enslaving addictions and shameless pratices that rob them of self-respect, satisfaction and hope. Addiction is a powerful force that takes hold first of the mind, then the body and ultimately the very soul of those who get caught up in it.

Not many people find a way out of serious addiction but Barry Woodward did. His powerful story, of despair and unexpected intervention is a message of hope worth telling.

A story is told from ancient Rome of a young girl who was placed on the public auction block. She was sold to the highest bidder. The girl was forced to turn around, front and back, so that the audience might see and make an estimate. The bids came in rapid succession, for she was young and strong. Finally one man outbid all the others; he bought the girl. He immediately put down the money and took possession of his property. The he turned to the slave girl and said, 'You are free. I have bought you freedom. You may go on your way.' She looked at him with her eyes wide open, with fear and apprehension. She did not understand. 'Free,' he said, 'You may go; you are free. I have given you your freedom.' The sincerity of his tone and the love in his eyes told her it was true. She fell at his feet, and, seized by gratitude, said, 'Please, I don't want to be free. I want to serve you. Let me serve you not as a slave but as a friend.'

I first met Barry when he was a student at Cliff College in 1998. It has been a joy to know Barry – he is genuine, humble, good-hearted and a man of integrity and honesty. Barry found the way out and chose freedom rather than slavery – and this freedom has transformed him so that he can fulfil his potential and serve his liberator as a friend.

If you have an addiction, Barry's story will inspire you to believe that you can be liberated. If you don't have an addiction, Barry's story will inspire you to believe that those who have addictions can be transformed. My desire is that Barry's story will bring liberation, healing and hope to many in our society who are addicted to behaviour that is dark and draining, and that they may also encounter the ultimate liberator.

J.John

Chapter 1

Needle Affliction

There's an old saying: 'Once an addict, always an addict' – but it's not always the case. I have known drug addiction, but I also know what it is to break away completely from that lifestyle. I've come a long way since the days when drugs, crime and prison defined me as a person.

I was once an addict, but now I am clean.

There was a time when I was as addicted to the process of injecting as I was to the drugs. I used to crave the sensation of the needle sliding into my arm, the buzz of the chemicals flowing into my bloodstream. There's a term for this craving; it's called 'needle affliction'.

Over the years I injected myself so many times that eventually the veins in my arms disappeared under my muscles. In the end, the only place where I could get a hit was in my groin; that's how bad I had become.

It's not a very glamorous image; but then, the life of an addict is far from glamorous. Beneath the bravado there is pain, broken promises, broken relationships, and a descent into a life of crime and deceit, often ending in premature death.

I was so addicted to drugs that even the high walls of a prison didn't prevent me from getting my regular fix.

Once an Addict

The year was 1985, just after the Miners' Strike. It was a Saturday, and I was lying on the bed in my cell in Strangeways nick, waiting for my girlfriend Lisa to come in for her visit. She visited me faithfully every day. My cellmate, Spike, was on the other bed. He was also waiting for his woman to come in. We talked about how quiet the wing was that day – unusual for a Saturday.

When we heard the keys in the cell door we thought it was time for our visit; instead, the door swung open quickly with an urgent whine from its hinges, and four or five screws ran in with two sniffer dogs.

'Right, lads – get up and get your hands in the air!'

We weren't going for our visit at all; we were being busted.

'What do you mean, Boss?' I said. 'What's happenin'? What have we done? There's nowt in here, Boss! We're straight!'

It was an automatic reaction: deny everything and show a bit of respect. We often called the prison officers 'Boss', to their faces. We now knew why things had been so quiet; they'd closed off the wing prior to doing the search.

'Don't move. Stand up. You're nicked!' shouted one of the screws.

They had us standing and waiting with our arms stretched in the air while the dogs were sniffing all over the cell – in the cupboards, round the chairs, under the beds, round each of us. It didn't take them long to locate all the other stuff we had hidden. We had needles, syringes, or 'works' as they are called, a spoon and some filters, all wrapped up in a tobacco pouch and hidden under the chair.

Then they searched us and checked our arms for the tell-tale track-marks that show someone has been inject-ing. The marks were there, but we still denied it. They didn't find any drugs because they'd raided our cell before we'd had our visit; but it was serious enough, all the same. They'd found the works we used to inject the drugs, so we would have to be punished. That meant loss of privileges and a spell in solitary confinement, and that meant no hope of any more drugs for as long as we were in there. The thought of not being able to get my fix was far worse than any punishment the system could throw at me.

I was in prison on remand and awaiting trial on a charge of possessing and supplying a Class A drug. I was 22 years old. I'd been using and dealing drugs for a number of years by this time. Before I'd got locked up I'd been living with Lisa on William Kent Crescent, one of the notorious Crescents or 'Bull Rings' in the Moss Side area of Manchester.

The Bull Rings were four crescent-shaped housing blocks linked together by walkways. They were populated by people who had originally come from that area, as well as students, drug dealers, petty criminals and people with mental-health issues who, under the government policy of the day, had been returned to the community. This last group were now trying to cope with their health problems outside of the institutions that had traditionally housed them. Together, the residents of the Bull Rings created a subculture of communal living. The backdrop to that culture was reggae music blasting from sound systems that could fill a room, carrying the dull thump of a base beat across the estate; then there was the gagging smell of urine in the stairwells and interconnecting walkways, the graffiti and dog litter, and the boarded-up windows that allowed us to live in subterranean darkness, day and night. Amongst this mix of people the appetite for drugs of all kinds was massive. I would get stoned in my flat with Lisa, and while I was under the influence of whatever drug I'd just taken, life felt good.

But things can go wrong very quickly when you're on the drugs scene. I had just sold some drugs to a guy, and as he was leaving my flat two police officers came by. Now this was quite unusual, because unless there was any real trouble, the Old Bill left us alone. But on this particular occasion, literally just as this guy walked out of the flat, these coppers walked past and they decided to come in. They didn't even have a search warrant.

They caught me red-handed. I had my stuff spread out on the table: scales for measuring out drugs, and the gear itself. They searched the flat, and I was arrested and later charged with possession of heroin with intent to supply.

Getting arrested was not a new experience for me. When I was 20 years old, I'd been put on remand in Strangeways Prison in Southall Street, Manchester. Usually when I got arrested I was given bail, and then I either got a fine, a period at an attendance centre, a probation order, or a conditional discharge if I was lucky. I wasn't sure that I would get bail this time. Being charged with possession is one thing, but being charged with possession with intent to supply is much more serious.

As it turned out, I was right to be worried. The magistrates refused bail and I was once again transferred as a remand prisoner to Strangeways. When I arrived there, I was taken through to the reception area where my clothes were taken away; I would only be able to use them again for court appearances. Then I was strip-searched and given prison clothing to wear. In those days remand prisoners were issued prison shoes, brown trousers, a brown jacket, a grey jumper and a blue-and-white striped shirt. I got one shower and a change of clothes each week. I became prisoner R06510 and I was placed in the holding cells. The new arrivals were kept there overnight before being placed in different wings throughout the prison. The next morning I was sent to the fourth floor of 'K' Wing – or K4, as it was known.

Doing time on remand was different to doing time as a con. On remand all you think about is getting bail. A remand prisoner will keep returning to court at different stages until they are sentenced or acquitted, but all they talk about is getting bail. Remand prisoners are also allowed daily visits, and visitors are allowed to bring in certain items of food and other luxuries for the inmates. If you are convicted and sentenced, it's a different story; then you are a convict, or a 'con' for short. Your privileges are limited, and cons like to talk about their EDR (Earliest Day of Release) or when they are due for parole.

My first visitor was Noel Proctor, the prison chaplain. He had a gentle, calming voice and a soft Irish accent. Noel used to visit all the new arrivals first thing in the morning before they were transferred to the wings.

When he first met me he asked me the same question that he asked all the cons:

'Does your family know you're here? Do you want me to contact them for you?'

'No thanks,' I replied, 'I'm all right.' I'd not had any contact with my family for about three years by this time; Lisa was my family.

Noel gave the new arrivals any help that he could, offering to come back later in the day when they were settled on one of the wings. Before he left he would pass each new prisoner an extra-strong mint. He called them 'anti-swearing tablets'.

I knew I could get food and toiletries brought in, but what really bothered me, much more than being arrested and put in prison, was how I would get my drugs. I knew that Lisa would be able to visit me every day, so we'd find a way for me to get my gear. These are the things you worry about when you're an addict.

They took me on to K4 and put me in a cell with a guy called Lennie. He was in his thirties and came from Glasgow; he had a long, ginger beard and long, ginger hair. He had recently finished a stretch of five years for attempted murder. He told me that when he got out of jail he went to the house of the judge who had sentenced him, broke in and slashed the guy's clothes. Now he was on remand for that offence; he'd only been out for a week.

Lennie had spent a lot of his life in prison and he had what's known as 'prison skin'. Anyone who's been in prison for a long time doesn't get exposed to very much natural light and sometimes their skin goes white; that's prison skin.

Lennie was a violent man and a drinker. He said he had a jacket with special pockets sewn into it so that when he was on the outside he could carry meat cleavers around wherever he went. He used to swear even more than the rest of us, and he was very aggressive – always complaining and getting narked with the screws, always on edge. He didn't make money from crime, he was just violent. Despite all that, I got on well with Lennie; we talked about things together – he trusted me and I trusted him.

Lots of guys find it hard to adjust to prison life. They get frustrated – especially the addicts. If you are used to taking drugs, the thought of having your supply suddenly cut off is very scary. A lot of addicts who end up inside get an appointment with the prison doctor early on; I certainly did. All you had to do was say that you were on the edge and about to boil over, and they would prescribe you something like Largactil, or 'liquid cosh', as it's known – an antipsychotic drug that calms you down and takes away some of the stressful feelings of prison life.

What I thought about most was the drugs I used to take on the outside – the street drugs that I could buy or get on prescription. Even in prison I managed to get a regular supply, thanks to Lisa. She'd pick up our prescriptions from the various doctors that we saw, and then she would do what she needed to do to get the money for the 'powders' I wanted. Having collected the drugs, she would put it all together and wrap it up tightly in a balloon or a condom, which she would hold in her mouth when she came into the prison to see me. She brought in Valium and DF 118 (an addictive pain-killer), and the thing I most wanted – my heroin, or 'brown', as it's called on the street.

In the visitors' room low dividers separated the inmates from the visitors. Lisa would come up and we would have our chat; we couldn't touch because of the divider between us, but at the end of the visit we would kiss and she would put her tongue in my mouth and pass over the drugs. We would get searched on the way back to the prison cells, so I would try to lodge the drugs in my throat. Occasionally I had to swallow the gear, hoping that the balloon or condom wouldn't burst inside me. After it had passed through my system, I would wash it and get at the drugs. Or sometimes, I would drink litres and litres of water until I was sick, and then I could retrieve the bag straight away. Using a blade that I'd obtained from a plastic Bic razor, I would split the bag open and get at my stuff for the day.

I was lucky to get any kind of visit at all. Some of the lads had no one. I remember there was a woman called Chantelle – I think she was a Traveller –and she would come and see some of the lads who wouldn't otherwise get a visit. On top of the visits, she would sometimes come within sight of the prison and shout over the wall, and then have conversations with some of the inmates. At times, when the lads asked her to, she would lift up her top and bare all for them. She was a very popular character around the prison.

In the next cell from me was a guy called Spike. Spike was about 24; he had blond hair and a long fringe, and he had tattoos on his hands. When his cell-mate got bail, I arranged to move in with him because he'd smuggled in some needles and syringes and a spoon – everything you would need to prepare heroin for use. Spike and I shared a love for drugs and so we got on well. His girlfriend used to visit him when Lisa came to see me. He was always wheeling and dealing, buying and selling; and he could fight, but violence didn't motivate him like it did Lennie.

Spike was a bit taller than me, and he came from Bury. He had a broad Lancashire accent, quite different from the sharper, more nasal twang I would hear in the centre of Manchester. He had bleached streaks in his hair and, like Lennie, he had prison skin. He was very thin and wiry-looking. He would look in the mirror and run his hand back over the fringe of his hair, pulling it back to reveal his receding hairline. 'I'm getting old,' he would say as he did this.

I now know that Spike never got the chance to grow old. He served his sentence and, within a couple of months of getting out of prison, he was dead from a heroin overdose.

Moving in with Spike was great for me. I wasn't able to inject drugs in Lennie's cell because I didn't have the works, so I had to smoke the heroin instead. Smoking was okay, but my favoured method was injecting; this was all part of the buzz.

On each wing, every floor had a prisoner who did the cleaning. Our cleaner was a guy called Bobby, who was from Skelmersdale. Bobby had a drawn face and hair that looked like it had been permed; I guess he was about 40 years old. In any prison the cleaner is in a position of power, because he can pass information and items from one cell to another; he's a good person to make friends with. Nobody knew whether to trust Bobby or not, but we had to rely on him to pass on and receive things from other addicts in the prison, and we had to pay him to do it.

One night he came round. Spike and I were getting fed up with him so we said we didn't have anything, and we sent him away empty-handed. The next day was a Saturday and, as usual, we were dressed up for a visit. If we could find a good pair of prison jeans that fitted well and were faded, and a decent shirt, we would keep hold of them and wash them in our plastic bowl in the cell rather than hand them in to be washed. This was our definition of 'best clothes', and visits were the highlight of our day; we wanted to see the girls and get our drugs.

But this time it had all gone wrong. The screws had been tipped off and had found our works – the needle and syringe we used to inject drugs and other paraphernalia. We knew that Bobby had grassed us up, and I think if we'd been able to get at him right then, we would have killed him.

Straight after they'd finished searching the cell, we got put in solitary confinement and we got no visits that day. When Lisa arrived for the visit, she was escorted to a holding area and strip-searched, but she guessed that something was wrong and she managed to swallow the balloon full of drugs, so they found nothing. She denied all knowledge of my drug-taking activities, and was sent home. They told her I had been 'nicked' and would not be able to see any visitors.

On Monday morning Spike and I were in front of the
Governor. We lost five weeks' remission; that meant
another five weeks added to our time in prison, if we
were convicted and given a custodial sentence. We were
sent to 'H' Wing, the solitary confinement block, for five
weeks.

Solitary confinement, or 'the block', as it's known,
was in the guts of the prison. In the remand side of
Strangeways, during the 1980s it was on the first floor,
actually the basement, of 'H' Wing – an area known as
H1. Each cell contained an iron bed, a bucket and a
washbowl. During the day I had a cardboard table and
chair, and at 6 p.m. I would come out of my cell, bring
out the table and chair, and take in a mattress for the
night.

Twice a day I emptied my bucket and got some water
for my washbowl. I had no contact with anyone else, no
radio, and no other privileges. I wore slippers in the cell.
Prisoners in the block had to go and get their food on
their own. I could see that Spike was in the cell opposite
me because he would peer through his spy-hole when I
went to get my meals, but I couldn't talk to him.

Visits were completely closed, so there was no physical contact with the people who come to see you. For any
inmate, the boredom of being in solitary is a kind of tor-
ture, but for me that was not the worst of it. Without any
access to drugs, I started to go through major cold
turkey. I was shivering, and there were goose-bumps on
my skin, like you see on the skin of a turkey that's ready
for cooking – hence the term 'cold turkey'. Also, the hair
on the back of my head stood on end and there was pain
in the back of my legs. During the day I'd lie on the steel
frame of the bed, tormented by hot and cold sweats, and
unable to sleep. I was hearing things, seeing colours,
thrashing about on the bed. The screws knew what I was

going through; they would tap on the door and shout things to torment me. I couldn't even have a smoke because we weren't allowed any tobacco. In the end I got so desperate for a smoke that I used the pages of a Bible as cigarette papers and tried to smoke the dust off the floor of the cell.

I was in H1, and above me, on H2, was the wing that held the sex offenders. These men were hated by other inmates and were put on a wing together for their own protection. They were the only people I could communicate with, and because I was desperate for a smoke I would bang on the ceiling, and occasionally the guy above me would drop me down some tobacco and matches, attached to a line – a strip of material about a quarter of an inch thick, torn off the edge of a bed-sheet and lowered down through the window of the cell above. To catch it, I would reach through the bars and put my fingers through the mesh that was fixed outside my window.

I did get one visitor whom I was able to see face to face: Noel Proctor, the prison chaplain, came to see me. He was still handing out the extra-strong mints; he knew we weren't allowed any tobacco in the block, but he could give us sweets. A lot of the inmates respected Noel; I certainly did.

After five weeks, Spike and I were put back onto the ordinary prison wing. When we got back there, Bobby the cleaner had been to court and had been sentenced; he was no longer on remand, so we couldn't get to him. During my time on the block I'd just thought about the drugs, and the pain and my craving. I'd suffered all this humiliation – carrying cardboard furniture in and out of my cell, smoking the dust off the floor, waiting for someone to drop me the stub-end of a smoke, suffering the trauma of cold turkey – and yet all I could think of now was where I was going to get the heroin I needed to function, the gear I loved so much. That was my prison, not the bricks and bars that contained me physically. I could be out on the street, and I would still be bound by it, driven by the need to secure my next fix.

So this was my life: I had my partner, and my flat, and I loved my music; but the most important thing in the world to me was my drugs. Getting my daily fix was the number-one priority for me, and I would sacrifice anything to get it. Forget everything else; what really defined me was the fact that I was an addict.

Chapter 2

A Good Start

I always tell people that I was brought up in a great home. The problems I've had in my life weren't caused by my upbringing. I had a good childhood and I got on well with my mam and dad when I was a kid.

I come from a working-class family and I am the youngest of three lads. My brother Shane trained as an electrician and now works as a supervisor in environmental health at Salford Council. My other brother, Kevin, trained as a painter and decorator and is still in that business today.

My dad is a typical Yorkshireman: plain-speaking, straight and honest – as genuine as they come. He was born in Stainforth in Doncaster, one of nine children, and his family really struggled for money while he was growing up. My dad's father and brother were both miners.

While my dad was still quite young, his father contracted a lung disease and had to come out of the pits; the family then moved to Main Street in Howarth in Yorkshire. My dad lived there until he went into the army, and it was while he was serving that he met my mam.

When he left the army, he moved back to Howarth and worked in the quarries, shot firing – breaking up the rock at the quarry face. He had all kinds of jobs. After he and my mam married, they moved to Salford, where she came from, and he was in the police for a while. He drove HGVs, and for a time he worked in a woodyard mending pallets. My dad always worked very hard, trying to make ends meet. He had a passion for sport, especially Rugby League. He played the game until he was in his forties.

My mam's family came from a similar background; she was one of ten children. Her dad was employed by Salford Council (or the Salford Corporation, as it was then called) in a builder's yard; he had started working there at the age of 13. During the First World War he was called up and fought in the Battle of the Somme. While he was there he took a shot in the leg and was invalided back home; then after a period of convalescence he went back to the builder's yard.

Like my dad, my mam had a number of jobs. She worked at the local fish and chip shop, and when I was a kid I would go up to the back of the shop and Mam would give me fish and chips to take home. She also worked for a catalogue company, and then later she worked part time for Marks and Spencer. Sometimes I'd meet her from the bus if she'd been shopping and help her carry stuff home.

My dad had a mate called Des. They played Rugby together and Des would organize New Year's Eve parties at the Golden Gate pub on Cross Lane in Salford. He was a real character. He had big seventies-style sideburns and sometimes he wore a colourful shirt, a tie and a white suit. He was a bit of a rough diamond, but just the kind of person you need to organize a good party. We went there year after year, together with a number of other families and friends. There would be drinking, music and dancing, and a comedian would come on. And then on the stroke of midnight we would all join hands and sing 'Auld Lang Syne'. These where great times, and they remind me that, whatever it was that went wrong with me, it wasn't because of my childhood.

Although I had a good family life, I really struggled when I got to comprehensive school. I was just not interested, and I was always trying to blag my way through. I used to copy others rather than try to do the work myself. On my first day there I had a fight. Some kid was riding on the back of a bike, while his friend was doing the cycling. They rode past me and the kid on the back of the bike spat at me. It landed on my face, so I ran up and pulled him off the bike, and we had a fight right there on a path outside one of the classrooms. It wasn't a brilliant start to my school career.

Some of the teachers used to get annoyed with me. During one music lesson I was sitting at the back talking to my mate Froggy, and the teacher, Mrs Lee, threw a blackboard duster at me, and it hit me between the eyes. It split my head open and I ran out of the class. I ended up in hospital with stitches in my head.

Once I got beaten up by one of the PE teachers for having a laugh with one of my mates in the gym changing-rooms. This teacher really did give me a beating; it wouldn't happen now. I told him my dad would kick his head in.

By the age of 12 I had started smoking. My mate Piggy and I would go to a place near the school canteen called 'Smokers' Corner' and we'd have a fag together there.

Sometimes my friends and I would play truant. One time we were on our way to a girl's house on Salford Precinct, and as we got off the bus our history teacher was getting on, and he saw us. The next day we were all called into the headteacher's office. We all tried to forge notes from our parents the next day to explain our truancy, but we were all found out and punished.

In the evening I would go to youth clubs in Salford with my friends. There was the Heights club, the Charlestown club, and Snoopey's club in Swinton. We went to different clubs every evening, and we would share bottles of cider and get drunk.

One time my mate Wriggers phoned me to see if I was coming out. I said that I was, and I suggested that we go halves on a bottle of cider. I put the phone down and discovered that my dad had been on the other phone listening. He was furious. He came running into the room where I was and gave me a slap, and then he stopped me going out that night.

My mates and I had a number of girlfriends, and some of us were experimenting with sex by the time we were 14. One of my girlfriends lived in the next street and sometimes I would go to her house at lunchtime.

I loved music. We would listen to funk and soul; both of these were popular genres around Manchester in the seventies. At the weekends we would go to parties. Sometimes my mam and dad would go away, so at times I'd have everyone round, and we'd have a party. There would always be lots of booze, and on one occasion a classmate of mine, a girl called Viv Dean, got so drunk that she fell and put her hand through a window. She managed to slit her wrist open and there was blood everywhere.

I liked to make things. I was really interested in mechanical stuff. When I was younger, still at primary school, I would go to the woodyard where my dad worked mending palettes, get some wood and make go-karts. Sometimes I'd go in with him in the morning and we'd have sausage butties with one of his workmates. I remember that one afternoon I went to the yard to get some wood to use as a seat for my pushbike. When I walked in, a big Alsatian dog jumped up and bit me on my ear. I had to go to hospital for stitches. One of the guys in the yard took pity on me and gave me some money so I could go and buy a seat.

My fascination with machines developed over the years and I decided that I wanted a motorbike. My dad took me down to Ipswich to buy my first bike. It was second hand and it cost £150. Once I had the bike, my dad took me out to some off-road places in the country-side where I could ride. I started to enter into competi-tions and found that I was quite good. After a few years I had over a hundred trophies for trials and scrambles. I even got a sponsor. I was always fixing bikes and mend-ing engines. I loved it.

While I was still at secondary school I got a job at a bike shop in the evenings and weekends, selling parts and doing odd jobs. I stacked shelves in a supermarket in Manchester city centre for a while. I didn't mind working because I wanted to have some money in my pocket.

In my final exams I took Maths and English, and I knew I had done badly. I didn't even go back to the school to find out my results because I knew that I had failed, and I didn't think exams were important. I came from a working-class background; my brothers had gone out and got apprenticeships when they had left school, and I expected to do the same. As far as I was concerned, exams were irrelevant. When I finished school, it seemed natural for me to do what I was inter-ested in, and so I got an apprenticeship as a mechanic with one of the main bike shops in Manchester.

During this time I also started to go to clubs and I got into drinking in a more serious way. I never got convicted for driving over the limit, but after a year on the road I lost my licence for a variety of offences like speeding and jumping lights. I didn't mind if I got into trouble. When I was out on my bike, if the police saw me speeding at night, I would turn off my light so they couldn't see my registration number and speed away without stopping. I just didn't care in those days.

Often when I was on the bike people would shout out, 'Give us a wheelie, Woody!' I'd just slip the clutch, pull the bike back onto the rear wheel and ride along. I could go for miles doing a wheelie.

In some ways things were going okay for me at this time. I got sponsorship from a firm called B. J. West motorcycles. They gave me two bikes and any spares that I might need. I remember going to London to get measured up for leathers and a helmet.

I loved the life that bikes gave me, but I was also getting into more and more trouble with the law. For the first time in my life I was arrested for fighting. There was a big gang fight in Eccles involving about thirty people, and fifteen of us got arrested.

I would do my work at the bike shop and then in the evening I would go to the pub. I had a mate called Bridgy and most evenings after work we'd go out for a drink. He was about seven years older than me. He was five feet ten and well built, quite stocky. He'd done some time in borstal when he was younger, and he was as hard as nails. He liked to drink but he wasn't into drugs. He had his own fencing business and he worked hard at it. He also worked the door at the Wishing Well, a popular nightclub in Swinton.

The Wishing Well was a bit of a dive, one of those places where the carpet is sticky with years of spilt beer, but it also had a reputation as somewhere you could go to get a girl. I went there every weekend for a while and it was always packed out. There was an old-fashioned DJ there called Rockin' Roy. Roy was a bit of a drinker, but he always did a good job, talking over the music and saying things to wind the crowd up.

During the week Bridgy would pick me up after work and we'd go to the Bull's Head in Swinton for a pint; then we would move on to some of the other pubs on the top road, just a few minutes' walk away.

I went to the pub for a drink and a laugh, but it was while I was there that I had my first experience of drugs. There was a small group of guys who would come in, and they would be smoking cannabis – or 'draw', as it's known. While my mates and I were going up to the pubs on the top road and maybe on to the Wishing Well, these guys were going into the centre of Manchester to the bigger clubs there. The idea of getting involved in the Manchester scene appealed to me, and pretty soon I wanted to join them.

The first time I smoked draw, I was laughing and my hearing became sensitive, and I felt as if my senses had been heightened. It was very different from the effect of drinking alcohol.

I got to know one of these guys. His name was Chris Taylor and he lived locally. He was 25 at this time and I was just 18 or 19. He was a short, stocky guy with dark skin and a moustache. He was always smartly dressed in LaCoste and Fila gear, which was pretty hard to come by in those days. Chris was a real townie, and the things he got up to sounded exciting to me. I used to smoke a bit of draw with him in the pub before he headed into the centre of Manchester. Chris was friends with another lad called Paul Fennon. Paul was a bit of a fun character, and he also dressed smartly, and although he was a bit taller than either of us, he walked with a bit of a hunched back. He had fair hair with blond streaks and a long fringe, and he seemed to bounce as he walked along.

Paul and Chris had another mate who we called 'Psycho'. He came from Salford; he had 'LOVE' tattooed on one hand, and 'HATE' on the other. They called him 'Psycho' because he would do anything for a laugh. He used to stutter a bit, and he laughed a lot while he was talking. Like Bridgy, he had done some time in borstal.

We would all go out and get drunk or smoke some draw, and then we'd usually manage to do something stupid on the way home. One time, we'd all been out smoking loads of draw and taking LSD, and we were walking home through a posh part of Salford. I think it must have been about 2 o'clock in the morning. We decided to walk through the back garden of a huge house as a short cut. The property included an indoor swimming pool, and we ended up walking through the door into the pool area. Psycho decided it would be a great idea to chase me round the pool, and then he pushed me in. I had to walk home with my clothes soaking wet.

This was 1981, and over the summer there were riots in major cities across the country. It all kicked off when thirteen black people died in a house fire in London. There were demonstrations to protest about what many regarded as an inadequate police investigation. At the time many people in the black community felt that the police were harassing them and picking on them unfairly; and all this contributed to the riots that we had seen on the news. Personally, I couldn't stand racism and I didn't like the police, so when I heard that it was kicking off right near us in Moss Side, I wanted to join in, and so did the others.

We went up to Moss Side and stopped off at Crispie's place first. Crispie was a Rastafarian who dealt in weed.

We got a taxi up to Crispie's flat and scored there; then we went on to a pub and smoked a few joints to get us in the mood for the riots which were happening just a few minutes away.

When we got there the riot was in full swing. The atmosphere was electric. There were thousands of people out on the streets in demonstration, black and white together. This wasn't a race riot; we were fighting together against the police. Some people were local and others had travelled in from other towns and cities to show their support. I remember chatting to a guy who had come from Liverpool. The police were there in full force, wearing their riot gear and shields and showing maximum aggression. The demonstrators and the police fought running battles amidst the noise. Over 1,000 people were laying siege to the police station. There were overturned cars and some shops on fire; you could smell the smoke; some people were looting. It was an intense, exhilarating experience.

The riots seemed to be well co-ordinated by key leaders from the Moss Side community. We followed the crowd of protestors and joined others who were attacking the police; the rush of adrenaline was amazing. We charged the police and retreated, charged and retreated.

After a while the riots began to ebb and we wanted to go into town before the pubs closed, so we decided to leave. We went into Manchester to a pub called the Union, still buzzing from the aggression of the riot and the effects of the draw.

Chris, Paul and I hung around together a lot and we became quite good mates. We would smoke weed and take whizz and generally have a good time. We were young and we knew it. We would go round to Paul's house when his parents were out and smoke loads of draw; if Chris's parents were out we would go there.

Often we would use a bong, a tall plastic pipe with a long stem, to smoke the cannabis.

After a night of smoking weed we would get the 'munches': smoking lots of draw gives you a craving for sweet things. Often late at night we would go to the local garage and buy loads of chocolate.

If we weren't out on the town we would stay in and listen to reggae music. Our favourites were Bob Marley and the Wailers, Burning Spears, Sly and Robbie, and Pete Tosh. We also loved dub music, a genre that evolved out of reggae and ska. In the afternoons Chris and I might go to the Arndale shopping centre in Manchester. We would hang out there, dressed in our tracksuits, listening to reggae on our Sony Walkmans and smoking a spliff. We thought we were the business.

Chris and I both had girlfriends; I was with a girl called Shelly. She was younger than me, and very trendy; she was about five feet four with mousy brown hair. Like the rest of us, she used to wear Slazenger jumpers – definitely 'in' during the eighties – and expensive trainers. She did okay for herself in the end, becoming a hairdresser at a Vidal Sassoon salon.

Chris's girlfriend was called Della; I had gone out with her before Chris. She had blonde hair and was really attractive. The four of us used to go to her parents' house when they were out.

I was young and confident, and I thought I had a lot going for me, and I was attracted to the idea of getting into the Manchester scene. I was buzzing with the lifestyle: the drugs, the music, the clubs. I thought it was all there for the taking.

In reality my life was on a knife-edge. I was about to fall away from the love of my family and the values they'd taught me over the years, and into the squalor and violence that defines the life of an addict.

Chapter 3

Out on the Town

Like a lot of lads of my age, I had some money but no real responsibilities, so I decided I was going to make the most of it and enjoy myself. I was still living with my mam and dad, and I'd recently found a job doing valeting for a car sales showroom. It paid more than the bike mechanic apprenticeship and that was good enough for me.

Together with Chris and Paul, I divided my leisure time between the pubs and clubs of Salford, including the Bull's Head and the Wishing Well, and the buzz of the central Manchester scene. As I started to spend more time in Manchester, and use more drugs, so I began to drift away from Bridgy. He liked a drink but he'd never touched drugs and as I moved into that orbit, he moved out of mine.

It was around the time of the Moss Side Riots that Paul and Chris introduced me to the Union pub. In those days, before it was refurbished, it was a scruffy-looking place perched on the edge of China Town in Manchester, full of interesting characters: prostitutes, thieves, dealers and various other intriguing individuals. The windows were cracked and yellow, darkened by years of fumes from all the draw that had been smoked there. We sat on green plastic seats that had been fitted to the walls. Over the years these had been slashed so that if the police 'dropped in', anyone who was dealing could stash their gear in the seat cushions, and remove it all again when the police had gone.

The manager of the pub was a black guy called Leroy. He was a bit camp but he was also a hard man and he carried an air of authority. Leroy ran the place his way, and everyone was expected to co-operate. He wore a big trilby, and under the hat he was completely bald. He was a laid-back, friendly character, very popular with the locals; he inspired a bit of loyalty in some of us. Occasionally there'd be a bit of trouble and Leroy wasn't afraid to step in and sort it. You knew he meant business when he took off his hat – that meant things were about to kick off. He was a hard fighter and I liked him. If Leroy got involved in a fight, I would steam in with him and give him a hand.

I got to know some of the regulars who came in there, including the prostitutes. There was Peggy; we called her 'Old Peggy', because she was in her fifties and still working. She had grey hair but it was always dyed. Like a lot of these women, she had a pimp who sent her out to work. She would come in every night high on amphetamine and looking for clients. She always dressed in smart but old-fashioned clothes and wore neat make-up. She was a kind and caring lady, despite her trade.

Then there was Sheila; she had two of her front teeth missing, but it didn't stop her from doing business. She was quite a large woman in her mid thirties, with short, streaky hair and a really bubbly character. She would work all hours to make money and give her daughter the best she could. She used to take amphetamine too, mainly in the form of a slimming tablet called 'Dospan'. This gave her the energy she needed to keep working. It finished her off in the end because she just used too much of the stuff over a period of time and died of a heart attack.

And then there was Maureen; she had permed brown hair, about shoulder length. She was easy to talk to, but she looked like life had treated her hard. She usually wore a fur coat, and she had a couple of kids that she thought the world of. She would come in to pick up clients every night, like clockwork; she was working just to make ends meet. When she was done she'd go back home to her family. She was a real working mam.

Sheila had a lodger called Irish Jim. In his late twenties, he was a petty thief. He was very skinny and had lots of tattoos. He would break into cars and do petty crime to make money for the evening. I know he'd had a tough time when he was a kid.

Under Leroy's management everyone knew what was, and what was not, permissible at the Union. You could skin up and openly smoke draw there without any hassle. If you'd been given the okay, and you were discrete about it, you could deal, but you didn't make a public spectacle of it. The juke box was a big old-fashioned thing that played 45s; it was always on and there was usually a big cloud of smoke hanging in the air.

For all its grime and sleazy atmosphere, I was very fond of the place; it was a comfortable place for us to meet together, have a good time, and relax. Often the Union would be packed, everybody just chilling out together, having a good time. The music would be blasting out, people were smoking weed, laughing and chatting; thieves would be in there selling knocked-off gear; there'd be some dealing going on, and the working girls would be popping in and out with their clients. Many of them were genuine people trying to make the best of life, and I counted some of them as my friends.

I began to spend more of my evenings in the centre of Manchester with Paul and Chris, but also with others from the Union. We would use a variety of drugs – LSD, whizz, draw – so it was inevitable that we would eventually come across heroin.

I remember the very first time I saw the effect that heroin can have on someone. Chris knew a guy called Steve Williams who lived near him. Steve was quite skinny and he was always messing around with cars. We went round there one night to smoke some draw and chill out a bit, and we met Steve's brother Tommy. We didn't even know Steve had a brother. Tommy was an old hippie type who'd really lived the alternative lifestyle; he wore old denims, a long baggy jumper and numerous bits of jewellery that he'd collected. For years he had lived in a teepee out in the sticks somewhere. He had long hair and he was covered in tattoos, some of which he had done himself – he had his own tattooing equipment. Around him was the familiar smell of petunia oil, a favourite with hippies. He was staying with his brother after just finishing a three-year stretch for burglary.

Tommy was from Bury in the suburbs of Manchester, and had the broad accent to match it. When we met him he was in his mid-thirties, and he had made the long progression from occasional drug use to out-and-out junkie. He was very mellow, very chilled; and he was always injecting, so that being an addict was now a part of his identity.

So we went over there one night to smoke a few joints and listen to some music. Steve had a good hi-fi system, and we sat in the living-room and someone rolled a spliff. And then Tommy came in.

'This is my brother, Tommy,' said Steve. We said hello and Tommy came and sat down with us.

'All right, lads! How you doing?' he said.

We said we were okay, and we chatted for about ten minutes. Then, right out of the blue, Tommy said, 'I've just had a dig of heroin.'

We were all taken back a bit but tried not to show it. Now that really made Tommy a mysterious figure. We were very curious about the effect it would have on him and so we watched him intently. He seemed relaxed; his pupils were small like pin-heads; and he explained to us what he had done. It didn't seem to affect him that much but we were intrigued.

A few weeks later, on a Friday night, we met at the house of one of the girls in our group. Her name was Julie Walker. The lads were all together; I think there were about ten of us crammed into a box room, just getting stoned together. The girls were in another room getting ready to go out. We smoked a bit of draw and listened to some reggae, just to get us in the mood before we went up town. Paul was out and we were waiting for him to return. When he did show up we could see he was excited about something.

'Hey, guys,' he said, 'I've got some heroin!' He'd obviously gone and bought some from whatever source Tommy used. Paul came in, sat down on the bed and took out a wrap of paper.

'You see this,' he said. 'This is heroin.'

By now we all wanted to have a look. Inside the little envelope of paper was a small quantity of brown powder. We all watched as Paul placed the wrap on the bed and took out a needle, a syringe and a spoon. He looked round at all of us.

'Who's having some?' he asked. We looked at each other, and then at Paul. There was silence for a moment.

'I'll have some,' said Chris.

'And me,' said another. Then we all wanted to try some – none of us wanted to be seen to be bottling it.

Paul carefully opened the wrap and divided the powder into ten equal lines using a razor-blade. He scraped off the first line into a spoon, added some vinegar and water which he had brought up from the kitchen; then he used the syringe to get the right amount of water. Then he took out his lighter and waved the flame under the spoon to heat up the mixture. When it had boiled he drew it into the syringe, then turned to Chris.

'You first,' he said.

'Okay,' said Chris.

'Use your belt as a tourniquet,' said Paul.

Chris took off his belt and tied it around his arm at the top, pulling it tight. He moved his arm up and down until one of the veins lifted under the skin. Paul looked at the syringe for a moment, flicked it to bring up any bubbles, squeezed it to remove any air from the barrel, and then pressed the syringe into Chris's skin, sliding the shaft of the needle into a vein, and injected the heroin into his bloodstream.

We all looked intently at Chris to see if there was any reaction.

'How does it feel?' someone asked.

'I don't know,' said Chris. 'I don't know how I feel.'

'Is it good?' someone said. Chris lay back on the bed and went quiet.

Paul repeated the process of mixing and heating the gear with the second bit of heroin, this time injecting himself.

As each of my mates took it in turns to be injected with the gear, I thought to myself, *This is serious stuff now – this is heroin. How is this going to make me feel? What will be the consequences?*

These thoughts came into my mind and then went again. I wasn't going to bottle out if all the rest of them were having a go. I was the last one to have some. I watched as Paul slid the needle into a vein in my arm, and I waited for the effect to kick in.

To be honest, I was a bit disappointed. After the opium hit my bloodstream I got a sudden rush in my head. That's why so many people prefer to inject, for the extra effect. After this there was a bit of a buzz to it, different from what I had felt with other drugs, but I didn't really enjoy it. At one point I felt sick and ended up in the bathroom, vomiting. Most of the time I kept my eyes shut, because 'H' makes you feel drowsy. I also felt itchy, another symptom of taking this stuff. We didn't go out that night; we didn't feel like it after our experience with heroin.

Addiction is a scary thing. You think you can handle it and stay in control, but you can't – and we were going to learn this lesson the hard way.

We were in the Bull's Head pub the next day, and we started to talk about what had happened. It turned out that none of us were that impressed. We talked about the rush being different, and that was enjoyable, but it seemed that heroin was not as good as the other drugs we'd had, and we had all thought the experience would be much better than it actually was. In the back of my mind I was telling myself that this had been a one-off. I wasn't going to take brown again.

We still had this sense of excitement about the fact that we had injected heroin. Some of the lads were keen to have another go; and one of them suggested we get some more. A couple of days later they went to Tommy's and asked if he would take them to his supplier in Bury. Tommy was happy to oblige, knowing he'd end up getting some of the gear. When the lads got back, we all had a keen sense of anticipation, and some fear – not that we ever showed that fear. We hid it behind our 'Jack the lad' attitudes. We all knew that heroin was addictive, but we didn't yet know what it was to be addicted.

Again we passed the gear around, all of us using the same works. Sharing needles seems reckless now, but this was 1982 and the whole AIDS thing hadn't really kicked off, and we didn't really appreciate the dangers involved.

After taking it the second time, I sat there feeling relaxed but I also still felt a bit sick. I closed my eyes and started to drift. *Yes*, I thought, *this is good. I can see why people like this. It's different, and everything is going to be okay. But I'm not having this again. This is the last time.'*

The day after that I didn't have any more heroin; I knew that some of the others had had some. And the following day, again I didn't have any because I wanted to stay in control. Then I got a phone call from Chris.

'Hi, mate. How you doing?'

'I'm doing great,' I said.

'Are you coming out tonight?'

'Yes. Where we going?'

'Well, my mam and dad are going out, so Paul and I said that we're going to stay in. We're probably going to go up to Bury to score some more brown. Do you want to chip in with us?'

I thought that since it had been a couple of days since I last had some, it would be okay, so I said yes.

And that night I went to Chris's house and we all injected again.

And two days later I had it again.

After the first four or five times of taking heroin, I stopped feeling sick. The nausea had passed and this made it more enjoyable. My system was getting used to the drug; I was getting resistant to it, and addicted to it as well. I carried on taking heroin over a couple of months, missing the odd one or two nights here and there and pretending to myself that I was in control. Then I noticed that, on the days after I had taken it I felt like I had a severe bout of flu; but as soon as I had some more heroin the symptoms would go. Before I knew it, I was taking it every day, both for the way that it made me feel and also to stop the withdrawals. I was well on the way to hard-core addiction.

If you'd challenged any of us about getting addicted, we would have denied it. We all thought we could handle it – we could stop it tomorrow if we wanted to.

I started going to the pubs and clubs in the centre of Manchester more often. Initially I used to go with Chris and Paul, but then I started to go on my own, hanging around with Irish Jim and other thieves from the Union. I had a friend called Deano from Salford, and he introduced me to a way of stealing from fruit machines that we called 'shackling'. Some of us would go out from the Union to various pubs in Manchester, looking for a particular kind of fruit machine. If the money slot was red with a light behind it (we called these machines 'red lights'), we couldn't do it; the slot had to be metal for the trick to work. We would find a suitable machine and then we'd use a piece of strimmer wire which had a little hook bent onto its end. We would put it down the money slot and click hundreds of credits onto the machine; then we would play it until it was empty. We had a system that always worked, from the way we stood round the machine to the way we played it. We found a number of places where we could do that, and we made hundreds of pounds that way.

One of the clubs we used to go to after the pubs had closed was Brewster's on Piccadilly. This club was full of football fans. I wasn't particularly into football, but my mates were, and we could have a great night out there.

The customers used to smoke a lot of draw and drink a lot of alcohol in there; it got pretty rowdy.

As I got more involved with illegal drugs, I decided to give up alcohol. Quite a few drug users do this, and those of us who stayed sober would refer to people who were drinking as 'beer monsters'.

Cutting out alcohol meant that if I got pulled up when driving, I wouldn't get nicked, and it also meant I would be able to keep my head if any kind of situation developed. I was out every night. I'd be in the Union and other pubs and clubs. By now I had even found myself some alternative accommodation, kipping on the sofa in a flat that belonged to a girl called Collette who lived in Hulme and whom I had met and befriended in the Union. If I wasn't at home I could stay with her. I would get back to her place at about four in the morning, and then I'd be up again a few hours later to drive to the car showrooms for a 9 o'clock start.

By now injecting had become my favoured means of using drugs. I was now injecting other drugs as well as heroin; if you could inject something, then I would. There were certain public toilets in Manchester that I would use, including one round the corner from the Union. I used to come out of the pub, go to these toilets and have a 'dig' (as injecting drugs is called) in the cubicles. I would then go back to the Union. We weren't allowed to inject in the pub; that was one of Leroy's rules. In fact, Leroy frowned on this kind of drug use.

At the time I was still trying to hold down a job, but I couldn't sustain that lifestyle in the long run. I'd get into work after being up all night, do some valeting, and then by mid morning I was locking myself in the toilet and falling asleep. No one seemed to notice my erratic behaviour; certainly no one commented on it.

I was also beginning to realize how much money some of my mates were making from thieving and dealing; so I left my job and I started to deal various drugs, thinking this would give me a better way of life.

Each night, before I went out, I would cut up the draw into different-sized deals and then wrap them in tin foil. Then I would go and sit in my spot in the Union, deal a bit, and then visit some other pubs and do business there. I had my own regular customers. I was also selling whizz; at weekends I would get hold of some LSD to sell to the gangs of lads who would come in to score before they went out on the town. I soon learnt that there was lots of money to be made from my new profession.

The main club I used to go to was a new club called the Haçienda. I was in there on the first week it opened in 1982. The first resident DJ was a guy called Hewan Clarke, who had a very distinctive music style; he played a lot of music imported from America.

The club had been converted from an old yacht showroom and made use of the warehouse layout – the industrial girders, iron pillars and high ceiling. The Haçienda was a very different place compared to most clubs in Britain, with their sticky carpets and potted plants. The Architectural Review called the Haçienda a 'pioneering interior'.

As you went into the club, there was metal plating covering the floor at the entrance. The sound system and lighting deck had been built into the infrastructure of the place. There were black-and-yellow painted steel posts rising from the floor to the roof, giving the place an industrial feel and a sense of urgency. There was the main room and then another, more intimate, chilled-out room downstairs. There was lots of UV light, and lots of booths where people could sit and chat or just watch what was going on.

The Haçienda was eventually forced to close, but it's difficult to overestimate the influence it had on the club and music scene in Manchester at that time, and on what later became known as 'Madchester', an alternative music style that spawned a number of bands. The Haçienda also had a huge impact on the British 'house' music scene.

The club's owner was a guy called Anthony Wilson who used to be a TV presenter with Granada. He also owned a record production company called Factory Records.

The sound system in the club was mind blowing. If you were on drugs and walked in, it just blew you away because it sounded so powerful. In the early days Echo and the Bunnymen, Big Country, New Order and the Happy Mondays played there – it was the essential venue in the city.

I'd go there six nights a week, every night except Sunday. I loved it; I felt like a real regular and also that I was part of something great. During the week it was quiet, but the atmosphere was amazing, like no other club. At the weekend you would get the 'tourists' in. People came to the Haçienda from all over Manchester and beyond, so on a Friday and Saturday it was packed. I would smoke a bit of draw and sell some whizz in there.

Once the Haçienda had closed for the evening, I might head for the Piccadilly Gardens, near the bus station – or 'the Dilly', as we called it – in the centre of Manchester. This was a bus station where I could catch up with some of my mates who had just come out of the other clubs. We would hang around there for a while, off our faces. From there I'd move on to places like the Reno, a night-club in Moss Side. Most of the people were black, with just a few white faces. They played a lot of reggae music, and the atmosphere was quite chilled. Sometimes a few of us would go to the local 'blues' – illegal clubs where you could finish off the night.

By now I was spending all my time in Manchester, even during the day. I would go to the Oasis indoor market and hang around with the guys I knew from the nightclubs I used to go to. These guys made a living from shoplifting; they were real pros, and they could make hundreds in one day. I would sell them drugs. There was a tattoo artist in the Oasis who would buy whizz from me. One time he paid me by doing a tattoo for me – a cannabis leaf at the top of my arm.

While I was in the Union I got to know a guy called Space, and he was a bit of a space cadet! Another out-and-out addict, he lived for drugs. He used to wear a denim jacket and denim jeans and suede ankle-boots. Space loved whizz, heroin and a variety of prescription drugs. He lived in flats on Salford Precinct and he liked to spend a lot of time on his own. He hardly had any furniture. We would sit in his kitchen in the early hours of Saturday and Sunday morning, listening to Jimmy Hendrix, absolutely whizzing off our heads. Space sold drugs so he could keep his addiction going. He only sold enough to make what he needed. He had a piece of rope for a belt; he would take this off and use it as a tourniquet to help him inject. If he needed some syringes he would go to hospital with his arm in a sling and pretend he was ill; then, when he was taken to an out-patient cubical, he would steal dozens of needles and syringes. This was before there were any needle exchanges.

I had one friend called Liam. Liam had been a student but had dropped out and got into the drugs scene; there were quite a few people who did that. Liam and I shared an interest in the same music. From time to time I'd see him in the Haçienda, and then we would go back to his flat in Moss Side where we would stay up all night taking speed, listening to music and chatting – usually talking rubbish, like you do when you're on whizz. Liam was an educated guy with a smart haircut. He lived in a simple, communal flat where each person had their own room and they shared a bathroom and kitchen. The drummer from The Fall had one of these rooms. Liam didn't just go with the crowd in the way he dressed; he used to buy his clothes from Oxfam and create his own unique style.

Then there was Matt. He actually worked at the Haçienda. He was always off his face on speed, and he used to chew the side of his lip. Sometimes after the club had closed we would walk back to his flat in Hulme and listen to music. He was a keyboard player and a sound technician. He didn't have a thing in his flat apart from posters from the Haçienda of bands that had played there, a few cushions, a mattress upstairs, and a basic stereo. That was it.

I had had quite a few one-night stands with various girls when I was out on the town; it was all very free and easy. And then Lisa came on the scene.

Chapter 4

Dealing Brown

I'd seen Lisa in the Union a few times, and on one occasion Paul specifically pointed her out to me.

'See her?' he said.

'Yeah,' I said. 'She looks all right. Who is she?'

'That's Lisa, Crispie's girlfriend.' I knew Crispie as the Rasta we'd scored off before the riots.

Crispie was a very sharp character: long dreadlocks, a white jag, and lots of gold jewellery. Originally from Yorkshire, Crispie's accent had now taken on a sharper Mancunian twang. Crispie liked to be dressed in the best designer clothes, and was on good terms with a lot of gangsters, or 'heads', as we called them.

Lisa was 31, about five feet four and very pretty, with long blonde hair, blue eyes and a slim body. She'd had her nose pierced before that was fashionable. She had come from a good home, and had then moved to Moss Side when she was a teenager. She would come to the Union to sell drugs for Crispie, but also as an excuse to have a night out.

I was in there on my own one night, smoking draw and dealing. I was just sitting at the table, and I caught her eye as she looked at me.

'What are you lookin' at?' she said, and then she laughed.

And I said, 'I'm lookin' at you,' and she laughed again. She was different, and I was definitely interested from that moment on.

Later that night she decided to check me out and so she asked someone who I was. She must have been happy with the answer she got, because she looked over at me again. I thought, *'This is Crispie's woman, but she's interested in me!'*

Collette was with me, so I asked her about Lisa.

'Well, she's with Crispie,' said Collette.

'Yes, I know that,' I said.

'But things haven't been right between the two of them for a while.'

'Oh, right,' I said, and didn't really think any more of it at the time.

That night I went to a nightclub, and I was surprised to see her there. I had been in this place a number of times before and I had never seen her there. I guessed that she had come because she knew I would be there. That night I gave her a lift home after the club had closed, and we started to see each other soon after that. Meanwhile she was still officially with Crispie.

Lisa had a friend who had a flat in St George's Court, near the Mancunian Way. He would let us use the place when he wasn't around, and after the clubs in Manchester had closed we'd go to this flat and have sex and take drugs and just hang out together. I liked her company because she was into all different kinds of drugs, just like me. I also knew that at some point I'd have to confront Crispie; but I didn't worry about that.

Over time I stopped going round to see my parents because I was always off my face on drugs and I couldn't face them like that. I still took pride in the way that I dressed but I had lost a lot of weight through drug use, and my face was drawn. I had simply stopped caring about anybody else except me. Drugs make you like that – self-centred in a way that means you never think about the effect that your actions are having on those around you, those who care the most – your family.

My relationship with my parents had deteriorated; they were getting phone calls from the police, and officers were turning up at the door asking to speak to me. My mam and dad's worst nightmare had come true – their youngest son was a drug addict.

I was round there one day when it all blew up between me and my dad.

'I can't understand why anybody would take drugs,' he said to me.

I looked him in the eye. 'There's nothing wrong with doing drugs,' I said. 'I'll always take drugs. I'll never stop.'

My dad was always good at hiding his feelings, but that day I could tell he was hurt. He looked away and shook his head in anger and disgust, and then finally he said:

'Of all the things in the world you could have done – all the things you could turn out to be – anything but a f****** – .'

He couldn't even bring himself to say the words drug addict. Finally he simply said, 'You're not my son any more,' and he walked out of the room. From that day on he disowned me, and I didn't speak to him for seven years.

At the time I didn't care. I just walked out of the house, got into my car and I thought, *It's time for me to live my own life. I don't need them.* It was a terrible attitude, but that's how bad I'd become – that's who I had become.

At this time I was still staying with Collette and Lisa was still with Crispie. She would get out whenever she could and we would meet up in the Union. She told me that she was getting fed up because Crispie was seeing someone else behind her back.

Lisa used to spend time with a friend of hers during the day, a bit of a crazy character called Irleen, and then I would see her at night. Meanwhile Crispie would sometimes be away for days on end.

Eventually there was a confrontation. One day I went to see Lisa at Irleen's house, and then Crispie turned up and was surprised to see that I was there.

'What are you doin' here?'

'I'm here with Lisa,' I said. There was a bit of a pause, and then Crispie said:

'What do you mean?' There was another pause and then the penny dropped. 'What?! You're screwing her, are you?' said Crispie.

'That's right,' I said, and we looked each other in the eye and I tried to keep calm.

'How long's this been going on, then?'

'About a couple of months,' I said. There was another long pause.

'You can f****** have her!' said Crispie finally, and turned to leave, giving us this parting shot:

'She'll only mess you around, like she messed me around!' The door slammed, and with that, Crispie was gone. I'd kept my cool, and I felt good about the fact that I'd stood my ground.

I was relieved that it was over; now Lisa and I really were an item. Up to this point I hadn't really worried about where I stayed, but things were different now; Lisa and I were together and we needed to get our own place. Meanwhile Crispie put all of Lisa's clothes in some black bin-bags and got rid of them; she couldn't go back there.

We stayed at Collette's place for a few nights and then in Lisa's friend's flat in St George's Court; and then we heard that there was a flat up for grabs in Meredith Court near the Game Cock pub in Hulme. The guy who had it wanted to sub-let it. This was the quickest way for us to get a place of our own; it could take months to get a place directly from the council. This would give us a base to deal from.

Meredith Court had a good reputation as a place to live. The flats themselves were nine storeys high, with a walkway that passed the doors on each floor. The lifts worked sometimes but they were slow and heavily decorated with graffiti. Sometimes the stench of urine made it almost impossible to use them. We lived on the first floor, so most of the time we would ignore the lift and just run up the stairs.

An older bloke had had the flat before us, and all the décor was really old fashioned. We wanted to make it our home, our 'pad', so we wanted it to be the best. One of the first things we did was to get my brother Kevin to decorate the flat. We went to Habitat in town for the wallpaper; we chose a trendy light-blue abstract pattern. We also put some new light-blue cord carpet on the floor. A friend of mine worked in one of the second-hand shops in Moss Side, and he had a Habitat-style suite in the shop that was as good as new, so we had that as well.

My customers who were shoplifters in town started coming to us to score, and this was very handy for when we wanted some nice things for our flat. People would come and visit us in the morning and ask us what we wanted. Later that day they would come back with exactly what we had asked for and we would pay for it with drugs. We had knife-and-fork sets in red from Habitat, ash-trays, plant-pots, pictures, a coffee-table – all matching, all top stuff. We had a top-of-the-range sound system, all separates with a ten-band graphic equalizer and four top-quality speakers.

We still spent a lot of time in the Union and it was around this time that I had the most extraordinary encounter I've ever had with another addict. There was a guy who I knew from the Union called Peter. He was in his late thirties or maybe early forties, and he'd lived in the area for years. He had black hair, a seventies-style moustache that covered the whole of his top lip, and a seventies-style haircut. He looked like your average kind of guy of his age. He wore jeans and denim shirts sometimes.

When he was younger he used to go in a club called the Twisted Wheel on Witworth Street in Manchester. The birthplace of Northern Soul, this club had been the place to be in the sixties, but it had been forced to close in 1971 because of drug use. Lisa knew Peter from her Twisted Wheel days.

One night I saw Peter in the Union; there was nothing unusual in that, and I thought no more about it. I was busy anyway; this was the weekend and the place was packed. People would come in to buy their draw and speed and LSD before they went out on the town. All night I had been selling and smoking draw, and popping out to the bus station to inject myself with speed every hour or so. Business had been brisk and I was off my face, as usual. Towards the end of the night Peter came over to me.

'Do you want to come back to the flat to do some drugs?' he said.

'Yeah, all right,' I replied.

We got in my car and drove to Beswick, near Grey Mare Lane Market, a five-minute drive from the Union. My plan was to go back to the Haçienda later. This is right in the heart of Manchester. We stopped outside 'Fort Beswick', a block of high-rise flats that had acquired their nickname because they looked like a military fort. The flats looked derelict; all the windows were boarded up and there were no lights on. We got out of the car.

'Come with me,' he said, and he led me through a door, and then up about seven flights of stairs to the top floor. I was thinking, *Where are we going? These flats are empty*.

The whole place was silent except for the echoes of the doors he was opening and closing, and the sound of our footsteps. I tried to keep up with him in the dark.

Eventually we got to the top floor and he led me towards one of the flats; he got a key out and opened the door. When we got in he reached for a switch and turned on the lights. I screwed up my eyes in shock. I don't know whether his flat was the only one with an electricity supply, because he had hot-wired it, or whether the whole block was still connected.

I wasn't surprised to learn that he was the only resident left in the whole block. He told me that they were demolishing the flats and he was refusing to move until the council offered him a decent place to go to. He led me into a small, bare room and then left me there for about five minutes in silence. I realized how much I missed the familiar sounds of urban life: thumps and muffled talk from people in other flats; car engines; shouting in the street or on the walkway. But here I was, in a place I had never been before, surrounded by silence.

I looked up as Peter came into the room again. He had changed his clothes; now he was wearing a karate outfit and a cap that covered just his skull.

'You want to have a dig of whizz?' he asked, as I stared at the clothes he was wearing.

'Yeah, man,' I said.

'All right,' he said, 'come with me.'

We walked into a slightly larger room. I guess it would have been the living-room, but there was no three-piece suite, no TV, just a sound system and a small settee; and in the centre of the room there was a big office chair, with a huge spotlight hanging directly above it.

Peter led me into the kitchen. He got out some speed, and we each prepared it for injecting; I used my own works, which I carried with me everywhere. Then I followed him back into the room with the chair. I sat down on the settee in the corner and he took his works and sat in the big chair with the light shining directly over him. I watched him as he lifted his foot and started to poke around at its sole, trying to find a vein. Peter had been using drugs and injecting for so long that the only place where he could get a hit was in the 'micro' veins in his feet.

I was mesmerized. This wasn't just a fix for Peter, this was an event. This guy dressed for the occasion, and he'd created a living space that was totally dedicated to the act of injecting.

I watched as eventually he got a vein and slid the needle in. Straight away he started to move around hyperactively, the tell-tale effect of whizz. I had a dig while I sat on the settee, and then I left his flat. This was an experience I will always remember. I don't think I have ever met anyone else who had so moulded their life to their addiction. He was the only resident left in those flats; the place was in total darkness, and Peter would sit there night after night in his big chair with the spotlight above him, injecting into the soles of his feet.

I found my way back down the stairs and drove to the Haçienda.

Lisa and I settled into our life together and went about the business of dealing and using various drugs.

Around this time Lisa introduced me to a guy called Joey Mason from Ancoats who had just got out of prison after doing a five stretch. Joey was in his late twenties and was well built and clean shaven, with brown eyes. He had a broken nose that was bent and slightly flat – a souvenir from some bother he'd had once. He was a hard man and he had dots tattooed on his hands. He also had an air of authority about him; he could command a bit of respect.

Joey was a heroin dealer. He didn't use it; he just sold it. He came round once with a sample for us to try, and gave us some good prices.

'Try this,' he said as he gave me a few grams, 'on account.'

'Okay,' I said, and I tried some of this stuff. It was good – very pure and highly effective.

'I'll have some from you to sell on,' I said.

Word soon got round, and we sold it in no time. I had sold weed, whizz and LSD before, but this was the start of dealing heroin. We soon learned that there was big money to be made; and the more brown we sold, the more we used.

Although I made a lot of money dealing heroin, I still had my principles; so, for example, I never sold anything to kids. When customers turned up and they wanted to score, if they looked too young I would send them away.

Getting prescription drugs was relatively easy because Lisa knew some doctors who would give you whatever you asked for. There was a Dr Khain, who eventually got struck off; and also Dr Castle, who later died. For £25 Dr Castle would give you virtually any prescription you wanted. At times we would get various morphine-based pain-killers that were usually prescribed to cancer patients. Sometimes we would also buy prescription drugs from the streets, such as Diconal and Palfium; both of these were extremely dangerous. With Palfium you could inject one tablet on one day and be fine, and then inject another tablet the next day, and it would kill you. Somehow, back then we couldn't see the risk.

By now people would come to us from all over the place, because there weren't many people selling heroin in those days. Even the guys from Salford were coming up to score. Chris and Paul had heard that I was dealing 'H', so they started coming. We also stayed in touch with Tommy, and he came over to see us; Tommy and Lisa had always got on well. One time we went over to Steve's house while Tommy was staying there, and he did a tattoo for both Lisa and I. We asked him to use the Rasta colours – red, gold and green – and to work these into a cannabis leaf. This was my second tattoo with a cannabis leaf on it.

These colours, and cannabis itself, are important within Rastafarianism. The colours come from the Ethiopian flag: red stands for the blood of the martyrs, green stands for the vegetation of Africa, and gold stands for the wealth and prosperity Africa has to offer. The smoking of cannabis – or 'ganja', as it's known – is considered a sacred act that cleanses the body and mind, and promotes peacefulness.

We did not consider ourselves to be Rastas but we respected the message of peace and love that Rastafarianism promoted. Listening to reggae music and smoking cannabis was a part of our lives.

Chris, Paul and the rest of the guys were coming to see me to score, but things had changed between us since the days when we were all mates together. That's what heroin does. You develop such a craving that you don't care what you do or who you cheat on to get it. We started as a group of friends who enjoyed each other's company and had a bit of respect for each other. But by now we were lying to and using each other, because the drug had taken control of us. People started to rob from their families, and the close bond that we'd had was gone; it was everyone for themselves.

Then the news came that Paul had died. He was the first person I knew who had died young; he was only 26. I was shocked, but it wasn't going to put me off using drugs. I was too wrapped up in myself to care that much.

At the height of my dealing I got nicked. I was living in Meredith Court, and I had all kinds of things going on. I got arrested and I was put in a cell for the week-end, waiting to go to court on the Monday to apply for bail.

At the time I was injecting every other hour, so it wasn't long before the withdrawals kicked in. I had never experienced anything like it before. As an addict, I was used to withdrawal symptoms. If there was a drought and there were no drugs around, then you had to go through withdrawals, but you could usually get some tablets to help you, otherwise you just had to do without. This was different. I was locked in a cell at Platt Lane police station – no drugs, no tablets, and no support. I thought I was Jack the Lad, with all my wheeling and dealing and putting myself about the place. I had all these nice clothes and all of my business going on. People were coming to see me to score; I was somebody in that neighbourhood. Even the people who hung around in Salford were coming to me, and that made me feel great. I had the flat, the girl, and the business. But here I was in a bare police cell with just a blanket; and the shivers were starting and the aches and the sweats, and I was getting goose-bumps on my skin – and suddenly I wasn't feeling so good about myself. I started to go through cold turkey. Not just the mild stuff – a really severe bout. I was seeing things, I felt totally sick, I was shaking and sweating and in pain. I just wanted to die.

About a day and a half into this, I was desperate. I was pacing around in the cell, and I went up to the door to look out of the sliding hatch. I remember vividly looking out into the area directly outside my cell, and I saw something – a creature – sitting on the floor.

This thing was maybe two and a half or three feet tall. It had a turban on its head and it was dressed in a white Arabic outfit; it looked like some kind of sheik. It was sitting on the floor preparing to inject itself.

One of its arms was just a thin bone; it had no hand or fingers. In the other hand it had all the tackle: it had a spoon, and it put heroin in the spoon, and then vinegar, and then water. Somehow it managed to light the mixture, and then it got a syringe and drew back the diluted heroin. I watched this thing through the hatch as it went through the familiar routine of preparing for a dig.

Wow, I thought, *it's got some heroin!*

I tried to call through the door: 'Hey, you! Just give me a little bit of that – just give me a little bit – please! Just save me the filter!'

As I was talking, a police officer appeared in the distance, walking towards my cell. I noticed him and shouted, 'Hey, Boss! Just ask it to give me some of that!' He was walking straight towards the creature I could see on the floor. It was still injecting, right there in front of my eyes.

'What are you talking about?' said the copper, and as he said this, before I could reply, he walked straight through this creature I had seen – and it vanished! I was devastated.

Where's that gone? I thought. *Oh no – I missed my chance! I could have had some of that. It would have stopped me feeling like this.*

I'd never been through anything like it. I would have sworn that this thing, this creature, had been right there in front of me, in the area in front of the cell door.

I managed to get bail on the Monday, and I got out of the place as fast as I could. I went straight back to the flat, where Lisa was waiting. When I got back, Joey happened to be there with a big bag of heroin. I was glad to be home.

Chapter 5

Cold Turkey

I went straight back to wheeling and dealing again, like I'd never been away. My luck didn't hold for very long, though, and I was quickly arrested again. I wasn't surprised to have my application for bail refused, and I ended up in Strangeways on 'G' Wing, the YO (young offenders') wing. I was still under 21 at the time. I went through reception and was examined by the doctor. Because I was going through major cold turkey, I was sent to the hospital wing. I was given a white gown to wear and told not to lie in my bed during the day. When I looked around, I saw that everybody was sitting on their chairs, except a few who were unable to because of sickness. Each morning I had to get up and make my bed. Then I had to sit on the chair by the bed and wait there until the evening, when I could get back into bed again.

My bed was right opposite the glass-faced room where the screws sat, keeping an eye on everyone. In the eighties you didn't get anything for withdrawals, just aspirin. My first night there was sleepless, as the pain of the withdrawal symptoms kept me awake. In the morning I was told that I had to make my bed, but not any old way – I had to use 'hospital corners'. This was the last thing I felt like doing, and when I made an attempt I couldn't get it right.

A guy on the other side of the ward came over to me; he was 45, with black hair and an Irish accent. 'You don't know what you're doing, do you?' he said.

'No,' I admitted. I felt terrible, like death warmed up. I couldn't concentrate and I couldn't get the bed-making thing right.

'Let me show you,' he said, and he helped me make my bed properly. I later found out that he was in for murdering his wife. They'd had a domestic in the kitchen and he had picked up a potato-peeler and stuck it in her side – a fatal wound, as it turned out. He knew he was going to be in for a long time, so he played up in order to stay in the hospital wing. He was street wise – an old-timer playing the system. I got on okay with him. There was a TV in the wing, and if you were fortunate enough to be at the end where the TV was, you could watch it.

There was another guy just a few beds up from me. He was about 24 with a thick head of light-brown hair. He was a traveller and when he was out of jail, he worked on the fairs. He was always talking, and he couldn't keep still.

Before my arrest I had been using at least two grams of heroin a day. I was given no medication while I was in the hospital wing. My legs felt like they had a heavy weight pressing down on them. I was in constant pain. I couldn't find a position that was comfortable. This was mainly because of the withdrawals but also because I had to sit on a chair all day. I was paranoid, I couldn't concentrate, and I was edgy. I was sweating, and my head was banging; my eyes were like saucers. I sat there all day; minutes seemed like hours; an hour seemed like a day. Then, when we could get into bed, I went through the same experience, only now I was lying down. I would lie one way, then turn over, then try a different position and then turn over again. This went on all through the night. There are only so many ways you can lie in a bed.

There was a clock at my end of the ward that didn't seem to move. I was given mild pain-killers, but they didn't get rid of the pain. For all that, I tried to stay in the hospital wing as long as I could so that I wouldn't have to go out onto the young offenders' wing. But eventually they moved me out because there was nothing more that anyone could do for me there.

I was put on 'G' Wing, on the fourth floor. I was still sick with the withdrawals, but I just had to do my 'turkey' and get my head down.

One morning, we had just slopped out and we were waiting for our breakfast; we got the shout for 'G4s' to come and get their food. When I got out onto the landing I noticed a few of the lads hanging around; it looked like they were keeping watch on G2. I had a view down to the landings, through the metal netting that was placed across each landing to catch anyone who jumped or was pushed. I could see that there were two prisoners fighting in the recess area. This went on for quite some time, and then they both came out, picked up their breakfasts and came back to the landing as though nothing had happened. The screws didn't see any of it.

In those days there were no toilets in the cells at Strangeways; you had to use a bucket during the night. First thing in the morning, the bell would go off and I would get out of bed, get dressed and wait for the doors to open. Then one of the screws would shout: 'Right lads, slop out!'

I would tip away the contents of my bucket – 'slopping out' – into one of the recesses. They always stank with the acrid smell of stale urine. Then I'd fill up a bowl with water for a wash after I'd eaten, then go down and get breakfast and come back to my cell. We all ate in our cells, with the doors closed again. Outside the cell I could sometimes hear the screws whistling, very tunelessly; the dull thump of other cell doors opening and closing; footfalls on the landing; and a bit of shouting from the other inmates.

I would eat breakfast, get washed, and about thirty minutes after that the door would open again and I would step out, put my tray out and go back into the cell, and a screw would bang the door shut. All our food was put on a heavy silver-coloured metal tray that we would pick up at the servery. We each got a plastic pint mug and a plastic knife, fork and spoon; we were given these in the reception area and were able to keep them in our cells.

We were in our cells until dinner-time, around midday. Like the other lads, I did whatever I could: read, sleep and listen to the radio. We would get one clean set of bed linen each week. I looked forward to receiving the clean bed-sheets: they smelt of fresh starch and felt nice to sleep in.

Then we were let out for dinner-time. We got our lunch and ate it – again, locked up in our cells. Then they opened the door, we'd put our trays out, the door closed and we were in all afternoon. It was the same in the evening, and then at about 8 o'clock a screw would open the door and the cleaner would be there with a big bucket of tea – this was called 'supper'. I would dip my pint mug in the bucket and take some tea. They put bromide in it to help with the guys' sexual urges; it helped to calm people down.

Every day we were allowed one hour in the exercise yard. Sometimes, if it was raining, they didn't let us out. Outside in the exercise yard, we would walk round in circles, and catch up with some of the other lads. The cock of the YO wing was a guy from South Manchester. He was about six feet two and quite well built. He had permed black hair. He used to wear his own clothes; you could apply to have your own clothes instead of the prison issue. He had a big, expensive sheepskin jacket that he used to wear during the exercise hour.

I knew that the best thing for me to do was to keep my head down, do my bird and keep myself out of trouble. Eventually I had my day in court, and they gave me a probation order and released me. I had done eight weeks inside. That may not sound like a long time, but when you're a smack-head like I was, every second can be agony.

When I came out of Strangeways I went back to our flat in Hulme. As I opened the door and looked at the place for the first time in two months, I discovered that all of the expensive stuff in the flat had gone. I never found out what had happened to everything. Lisa told me she had been staying away, but I often wondered whether she had sold it.

It may not have been Lisa, of course; there was a woman who lived on the same estate called Ilene. She was an old Moss Side villain who was now in her sixties with a family. The thought crossed my mind that she might have got them to burgle the place because she knew I was away. I never found out for sure.

Joey heard that I was out, and came round to see me. He brought a new type of heroin with him, and he gave me a sample to try. So while Joey was there I injected myself with it, and because I hadn't had any for a while it was too much for my system and I OD'd. I went blue in the face and my eyes rolled into the back of my head. Any heroin dose has the potential to be fatal. In our naivety, in the drugs world, we thought the best thing was to put the person in a bath of cold water and inject them with salt water in the hope that this would bring them round. Joey freaked out because he had never seen anything like this before, but Lisa was there and she knew what to do. She ran into the bathroom and turned the cold-water tap on full, then she told Joey to slap me in the face.

So Joey started slapping me as hard as he could to bring me round. Lisa shouted from the bathroom, and Joey picked me up, carried me into the bathroom and threw me into the bath fully dressed. I remember coming round with all my clothes on. I was shivering, but at least I was still alive.

People knew they could get their drugs from us, but because we were making good money some people started to get jealous, and that made us targets for other criminals. One night we really got caught out. We'd just had a visit from a guy called Stuart who lived in our flats and was also a dealer. I forget why he dropped by, but we had a chat and then he went off. Five minutes later there was a knock on the door.

To maintain our own security, we had a certain code for letting people in. When the building's security system was working, people could ring the buzzer three times, and then we would let them into the building. Then they would come to our door, knock three times and shout out who they were. Everyone we sold to used this system, and if we didn't hear the knocking we wouldn't open the door; it was as simple as that. If the security system wasn't working, people would just come straight to our door, but they would still have to knock three times and say who they were.

On this occasion Lisa went to the door and, thinking it was Stuart because he had just left, she didn't check by asking the person to shout out their name. She opened the door, expecting to see Stuart, and instead five guys ran into the flat – four black men with balaclavas on their heads and one white man with his head uncovered.

I was in the living-room with the drugs down the front of my trousers, where I normally kept them, and Lisa ran in, followed by these five guys, all brandishing baseball bats and knives.

One of them looked at me. 'You! Get into the f****** bedroom!' he shouted. Two of them kept Lisa in the living-room while the other two helped bundle me into the bedroom.

'Give us your drugs! Give us your money!' He was waving a baseball bat at me as I stood on the bed.

The guy without a balaclava seemed to be in charge. He was asking Lisa where the drugs were, whilst one of the other blokes continued shouting at me:

'Stay there, don't move! Where's your drugs?'

'I've got no drugs! I've got no drugs! I just sold the last bit!' I lied.

So the guy started hitting me with the bat while the other members of the gang started to rush around the flat, tipping things over, looking frantically for the drugs. Then the white guy pushed Lisa into the bedroom and started beating her.

'Tell us where your f****** drugs are!' he said.

'All right, all right! You can have them!' I could cope with them hitting me, but when they started on Lisa, that was it. I pulled out one bag of drugs from my trousers. I had more but I hoped this would satisfy them.

'There's the f****** drugs! That's all I've got!' I shouted.

One of the black guys picked up the drugs and they all ran out of the flat. I knew that the gang leader was called Ryan because the others had used his name. I didn't know him, but he sounded like he came from Manchester.

As soon as they'd gone I spoke to Joey, my supplier, and told him I'd been done over, or 'taxed', as it's known. We thought it might have been just a random hit, but then the next day another dealer who lived near me got raided by the same gang. This made it more likely that these guys were targeting the dealers in Hulme, and of course this reflected badly on Joey.

Two weeks later the same gang visited another couple who were dealers: Marcus and Bonnie, who sold a lot of draw, usually by the kilo. This time Joey was in the flat with Marcus and Bonnie when they burst in. They pinned Marcus, Bonnie and Joey to the ground. Again there was one white guy, referred to as Ryan, and he didn't have a mask on. He was the one doing all the talking. He hit Joey and told him to lie flat with his face to the floor; this time he had a shotgun.

While Joey was still on the floor they ransacked the place, demanding to know where Marcus and Bonnie kept their drugs and money. At some point Joey looked up and managed to get a good look at the guy called Ryan; Ryan saw this and kicked him in the face.

The next night Joey was out in a van with a crew tracking them down. That was the last we heard of them; I heard a rumour that they moved right out of Manchester and never returned.

Chapter 6

Dead on Arrival

While we were in Meredith Court we didn't pay many bills. That sort of thing wasn't very high on our priority list; and we thought that because we were paying the old guy rent, it was his responsibility. While I was in Strangeways the electricity got cut off; so in a letter from prison I told Lisa that she could get it hot-wired and who could do it for her. There is a way of wiring the electricity which bypasses the meter. So we used electricity without it being metered for some time, but then eventually the electricity board disconnected us again, only this time from the mains supply outside the building, and this left us without any power. About the same time our landlord wanted us to move out, so our time in Meredith Court was coming to an end. Once we'd moved out of the flat we scaled down our level of dealing, because the flat had been our base, and it was much more difficult for us to operate when we were lodging with other people.

We stayed with a couple called Trisha and Dan who lived in Hulme; they let Lisa and I sleep on the sofa. Dan used to play acoustic guitar, and he liked to smoke a bit of draw. Lisa had known them for some time because she had lived just over the road from them. They were a really nice couple, and it was typical of their generosity that they offered to put us up when we had nowhere to stay. They lived in a maisonette on the second floor of a two-storey block, and they had two kids. Dan was about 35, and very thin; illness had left him with light-yellow coloured skin. He had shoulder-length black hair that was usually a bit greasy and a moustache, and he walked with a bit of a stoop. He loved the music from the sixties. Most nights after Trisha had put the kids to bed, he would smoke draw and just play his guitar while singing; he had a great voice. His dress sense was a bit sixties too; he was a bit of a hippie. We would sit with him and get stoned while we listened to him play. The house was always cold because they never put on the heating.

Trisha was a bubbly character. She liked to wear jeans and long jumpers that came to the top of her knees. She had short hair that wasn't always washed; she almost had a bit of a punky look about her. Dan couldn't work because of his illness, so they tried to get by on benefits. They were honest, good people and they never stole things. We slept on the sofa each night, and gave them a little bit of money each week for food and lodging. The extra money came in handy for them.

Around the corner from Trisha and Dan's was a guy called Manny. He was about the same age as me – 21. Manny dealt draw and LSD, and he also used a lot of LSD. He was a bit strange; I think he'd had a really bad experience when he was tripping one time, and that had messed up his mind. He liked to talk in riddles, so sometimes it was difficult to understand what he was on about.

Manny was serious and calm most of the time. He liked to wear colourful tops, and a long raincoat. He was into the idea of Yin and Yang, and Feng Shui; and his flat was decorated in an oriental style. He had a low coffee table with cushions around it and he used low-lit lights to create an atmosphere. To enhance the effect, one of his lights was placed behind an oriental paper umbrella. There was always some Brian Eno or Captain Beefheart playing in the background and some joss-sticks burning.

We would often go to his house to swap weed for whatever drugs we had; sometimes we would get LSD from Manny. We could go to his flat to score and then sit round his Chinese-type coffee table and have a joint with him, and listen to some music. It was an experience just being in the flat with him.

At this time we were still selling a few drugs, but on a smaller scale than when we were in Meredith Court. We still had a big heroin habit and we were using other drugs as well, so we started doing other things to get some money to buy all the drugs we needed.

The main thing we did was shoplifting. I knew lots of other people who used it as a way of feeding their habit, so we decided to try it as well. One of the things about shoplifting was that it was only a minor charge, so if you got caught, the chances of getting bail were high; and because I already had a string of offences, this was the easy option. I had already done a bit of shoplifting in the past with some of the guys from Manchester, so I knew how it was supposed to be done.

The downside to shoplifting is that there's a high risk of getting caught. Because of my regular arrests I would occasionally spend the night in the police cells and also in the CDC, the Central Detention Centre. The CDC is in the centre of Manchester and is a kind of holding area for criminals who had been arrested. People can be kept there overnight or over the weekend before they are up at court. It was a horrible place. All the windows were in the roof, and there were no open visits; and it stank of cheap disinfectant. In fact the stink was so strong that you could tell if someone had been in there over the weekend, because you could smell it on their clothes. I don't know why, but I was unlucky and I tended to get arrested on a Friday, so I would end up in there all weekend, going through cold turkey.

One time after I had been released from the CDC, I went to score with a guy called Ratty. He was a top shoplifter from Hulme; he used to make hundreds of pounds a week. I used to sell heroin to him when I was dealing in Meredith Court, but now he had started dealing, so I was buying from him. I had £25 in the breast pocket of my shirt, under the jumper I was wearing. When I got to Ratty's house I was pleased to see he was in.

'How you doin', mate? Got any heroin?' I said.

'Yeah, come in.'

So I went in, and through to his bedroom; he wanted me out of the way of his girlfriend who was in the living-room. He got out his gear and told me that he had some really pure stuff that was uncut. He didn't have much, so he was only able to give me an eighth of a gram, but he said he was waiting for a new batch to arrive from his dealer. He suggested I have the eighth and then come back for more later. I was after a quarter of a gram of heroin, and in those days that cost £25. He said he could give me an eighth, so he weighed it out and gave it to me. I took it, prepared it in a spoon and injected it. Because I had been in CDC all weekend and the 'H' was uncut, I OD'd on it and passed out. Usually I would inject £25 worth in one dig, and I could do that several times a day without any problems; that kind of routine was normal for me.

I woke up at 1 o'clock in the morning in hospital on a trolley, while being wheeled down a corridor, with a nurse looking down on my face.

'Do you realize you're lucky to be alive?' she said.

'What d'you mean?' I replied. I was confused and disorientated.

'When you came in tonight you were DOA. You know – dead on arrival! The paramedics found you in a phone box and by the time you got here you were dead.'

I felt awful. I had bruises all over my chest from the defibrillator they had used to administer the electric shocks that brought me back to life.

They discharged me from the hospital, and I still had the £25 in my pocket, so I went back to Ratty's house to ask for my other eighth.

When I knocked on the door he wasn't pleased to see me. 'What are you doing round here?' he said.

'I've come back for my other eighth.'

'Don't you come knocking on my f****** door!' he shouted. 'You came round for gear earlier tonight and you didn't have enough money to pay for it!'

'No, Ratty, I had the money!' I protested. 'It was in my pocket – here.' I showed him the £25.

'You didn't have that before,' he said. 'We searched you and you didn't have any money.'

I began to piece together what had happened. I had been in the flat, did an eighth, and then OD'd. While I was lying there dying, they searched me but didn't find my money. Apparently another guy turned up around this time; he too had come round to score. The pair of them carried me to the phone box, left me there and then phoned for an ambulance.

You might think that this would have caused a rift between Ratty and me, but it's all part of life as an addict. There was nothing personal about it; I went back to Ratty and bought gear again many times.

There was one time when we were making money with stolen credit cards. We would buy them from pickpockets, or 'dippers', as they are known, and then prepare them to be used. I would use masking tape to cover the card and then use brake fluid to 'clean' it, and then I would sign it. There was good money to be made at this, but if you got caught you would be charged with forgery; and that was more serious than a shoplifting charge.

Sometimes if things weren't going so well, I would go into Marks and Spencer on Salford Precinct to find my mam. I knew she was working there part time. I will never forget the look on her face when she saw me. I wouldn't see her for months, and then I would turn up where she worked. One time she couldn't even recognize me, I was so thin.

'Hi, Mam. How are you doing?' I'd say. 'Can you give me £25? I've got no food.'

She didn't tell my dad she had seen me; she would give me £25 and, of course, I'd go and spend it on drugs. Then I wouldn't see her for another two years. That was how things got; that's it when you're an addict – you don't care where the money comes from. Steal it, lie for it, whatever it takes – so long as you get it. That's how addicts treat the people around them.

Lisa and I were okay while we were staying with Trisha and Dan; but like all these things, it didn't last. I'm sorry now that we did not treat them with the kindness they had shown us. One Christmas time they went away and we broke the lock on their electricity meter, took the money out, and glued the lock back up. When they came home we had left. We took the money and scored heroin with it. I am not proud of what we did, but that's how we were then.

After leaving Trisha and Dan's place, we moved in with a woman called Jackie who lived on the Bull Rings. Lisa had known Jackie for years. She'd had lots of relationships; some of them had been quite abusive. She used to take amphetamines like we did, and then, to get attention, she would pick holes in her face with a pin. One night Jackie was in her bedroom speeding, and we stayed up all night. In the morning she came out of her room and it looked like she had two black eyes.

I said to her, 'What's happened to you?'

'What do you mean?' she said.

'Your eyes!'

'I've been picking blackheads out of my face all night,' she said.

This became a regular thing that she did to get attention; it was horrible.

One time Lisa and I had a row and she moved in with a woman called Silvia who lived just up Ashton Old Road. I found out and went to see her. We got back together and I moved in. Lisa and I slept in a single bed while we were there. Silvia was about 38 and she had lived a bit; she was as hard as nails. She had shoulder-length, bleached, blonde hair and she was stocky. She had a few tattoos on her arm, two of which had been removed, leaving her with permanent scars. She was going out with a black guy who only used to come round when she had money to give him. We didn't stay there long. I felt uncomfortable in the place and I told Lisa we were leaving.

Meanwhile life went on; we were still regularly visiting the bent doctors that we knew; Dr Khain would give us both our prescriptions for Valium, DF 118 and temazepam. Twice a week we would go to the doctors in the morning, get our 'scripts', then go to the chemist. We would then take ten DFs and ten Valiums each, all at once. This would get rid of the withdrawals while we went into town to make some money.

Inevitably, the drug abuse took its toll on our bodies. Once Lisa got an infection from injecting into her bum.

This infection turned into a thing the size of a tennis ball. She had this for months and she had to live with it until it died down.

Another time I got an infection in my hand and had to go to hospital with it. I had injected into the back of my hand, and it swelled up like a balloon. I was in hospital for four or five days.

On another occasion, after getting out of the police cells after being in for the weekend, I got home and injected some Mogadon sleeping tablets because I was so desperate for a dig. It made my face burn and I thought my head was going to explode.

Even though I was an addict, there were some principles that I lived by. For example, I would never let Lisa take the blame for anything. If we were both caught stealing, I would always say that it was me. We would lie until we were blue in the face and I would take the blame, whatever the evidence. I may have been a drug addict but I still felt I had some dignity.

There was, however, one occasion when this principle didn't apply. Over time I built up a string of charges and convictions; I had been in Strangeways, and I was still only just into my twenties. Lisa and I got arrested again, and we knew that if I took the rap, I would get time.

I looked at Lisa and breathed out a long sigh. 'If I take the blame for this,' I said, 'I'm going to go down.'

'You don't need to,' she said. 'I'll take the rap this time; they're much less likely to put me inside for it.'

I had to admit this was true. Before Lisa met me she had already been charged with various offences, and she had served quite a few prison sentences, including a spell in Styal women's prison. But that was all a long time ago. Her more recent record was good, so it was much less likely that they would send her down. If we could both avoid jail, then we could stay together and support our habit together.

I struggled with this because, as I've said, I didn't think it was right that a woman should ever take the rap; it just wasn't done. We talked it through and in the end I reluctantly agreed that she should take the blame. Neither of us thought that she would be refused bail.

Unfortunately, we were both wrong. She was sent to Risley in Warrington, on remand. That really knocked me for six because we weren't expecting that at all; I was used to having her around and us working together. She was there for about six weeks, and I was really pleased to be back with her again when she got out.

While Lisa was in prison I decided that we really did need a place of our own again; so as soon as she was out, we went to the housing office in Moss Side. They offered us a flat on the Bull Rings, on William Kent Crescent. We decided to take it and we moved in and made the place our home. We continued to make our money to fuel our drug addiction by shoplifting and various other crimes, and from time to time we sold a few drugs, and life returned to normal.

Chapter 7

Caught and Convicted

By early 1985 I was on bail for six shoplifting offences. By this time I had been found guilty of seven other shoplifting charges, and one charge of using threatening or abusive behaviour.

I knew it was only a matter of time before I was sent down. When you're living this kind of life, it's inevitable. Eventually the criminal justice system lost patience with me, and when I was arrested and charged with possession of heroin with intent to supply, I was remanded in custody. I was sent to the remand section of Strangeways prison, and into the environment I have described in the first chapter of this book.

When my case came up I was taken to Court Number 1 at Manchester Crown Court, and charged with six counts of theft and one count of possession of a controlled drug. I had managed to get the charge of possession of a Class A drug *with intent to supply* down-graded to simply possession of a Class A drug.

Even though I pleaded my innocence, I was found guilty of the charges, and received a twelve-month custodial sentence. In those days you did three quarters of your sentence; so that meant nine months minimum. I had already lost five weeks' remission when Spike and I got caught with the works in our cell, so I'd have to do ten months and one week, minimum, if I behaved myself.

I returned to Strangeways not as a remand prisoner, with the privileges that that brings, but as a convicted prisoner, or a 'con'. As the judge passed sentence I felt like I had quite literally been gutted. I now understood this term in its truest sense because I just lost my stomach; it felt empty, and I felt sick, absolutely awful! I tried not to show it. I put on a good front. When I was taken down below the courtroom for return to prison, I tried to act as if I wasn't bothered. I wanted people to think I was hard enough to take the punishment, but really the thought of being locked up for even longer was overwhelming. No drugs. I could get drugs in prison but not the quantity I could get outside; and of course, there would be no sex for months! The only consolation was that some of the other remand prisoners who had travelled in the 'sweat box' (the form of transport used to take prisoners back and forth to prison) with me from Strangeways had received longer sentences.

Junkie Paul was one. I knew him on the out; he was from Moss Side and he'd lived in Hulme for a while. He had got four years. It made me feel better to think that he had received a longer sentence than me.

When I got back to Strangeways I was taken to another reception area and strip-searched again. This time the prison-issue clothes were blue: blue jeans, a blue jacket, a blue-and-white shirt, and a grey jumper with a blue rim round the collar. I put them on and they didn't fit properly – the jeans especially were too short. But this was prison, not a trip to the local sports shop, so I just had to get on with it. I put my own clothes back in a box. These were the clothes that I had got arrested in, and they had been unwashed for weeks. Now they stank of disinfectant and cardboard. The cells that hold defendants in police stations and the courts stink of disinfectant, so some of it rubs off on your clothes.

There would be no more daily visits from Lisa, no outside food, no speculation about getting bail; and just one visit every month. This was it. Bird. The atmosphere on the 'main' was different to that on the remand. It was much more tense. Here everybody was doing time and everyone was edgy, like a bomb waiting to go off.

In those days Strangeways had a reputation for being a bad prison. It was a typical Victorian jail, as they are usually portrayed on TV and in films. It opened in 1868 and shortly after that it was licensed as a place of execution when this was the law. Entry to the prison was through an imposing gatehouse structure which then led to two radial blocks: one for convicted prisoners with wings lettered 'A' to 'E', and the other for remand prisoners with wings lettered 'G' to 'K'.

A thick, high wall runs around the perimeter of the prison and the whole complex is dominated by a brick tower, some seventy-five metres high. It was usual to share a cell with one or two other men, even though at two metres by three and a half, they were designed to house just one prisoner.

I was allocated to a cell on 'A' Wing, on the fourth and highest floor. I shared the cell with a guy called Mike from Milton Keynes and my old acquaintance Junkie Paul. He had been sentenced at the same time as me, but for a longer stretch than I would have to do. The cell was cramped and tempers were frayed. We all had to live with the smell of each other as well as the residual stink of stale smoke and old carbolic soap which Junkie Paul had brought with him from reception. The walls were yellow but with a grey, institutional hue built up over the years. There were three beds: one single bed and one bunk bed. Mike from Milton Keynes had the single bed; he had been there about one month. Junkie Paul took the bottom bunk and I ended up on the top bunk.

I remember lying there, thinking, *It's going to be ages before I can have another fix*. I spoke to Junkie Paul about it:

'How easy is it to get brown on this side of the prison, here on the main?'

'Well,' he said, 'you can get it but it will cost you.'

'How much?' I asked, hopefully.

'Well, that depends on how much you want,' he said, and smiled.

I could hear the footsteps of other cons and the screws on the landing outside the cell, the sound rising and falling away as people walked past the cell. A bit of natural light filtered in from a Perspex window. They used Perspex so that the inmates couldn't use the glass to make a weapon and do either themselves or others real damage. Outside the Perspex, you could see the original iron window-bars, about five and a half inches apart.

The routine was pretty much the same as when I'd been on remand. We made our beds and settled in; then at teatime the keys clattered in the lock and the door swung open.

'A4s!' shouted the screw.

I followed the lead of the other prisoners and together we walked down to the end of the landing, and then down a spiral staircase at the edge of the central hub, with its huge domed roof. At the centre of the hub on the ground-floor level was a highly polished steel floor called the circle; I could see the design cut into the metal as I walked down the spiral stairs to the servery. The cons were not allowed to walk across this flooring, only round it.

I walked down to the bottom floor and under the domed roof to where the servery was, in the basement of the central hub. As I looked up from the servery I could see through the patterns in the underside of the circle, and the domed roof far above that.

In the servery, there were several long metal hot-plates lined up with the food served on each one. Behind the servery a row of about eight cons, all wearing white, would dish up the food. There were also a number of screws, again dressed in white, at the end, making sure each of the prisoners got no more than their portion. After I had queued and got my food, I walked to a line of big tea-urns and filled my plastic pint mug, which I had been given at reception that morning. Then I followed the other cons back up another flight of stairs on the opposite side and then eventually back up to A4. Same routine, every day: I'd get back to my cell with my tray of food, the other two would join me if they weren't already there, and then a screw would come along and bang us up.

Over the landing was another guy I knew called Micky Burns. Micky was an associate of mine from Moss Side; he was doing five years for armed robbery. After about a week, I managed to get a space in the same cell as Micky. I was well pleased – and not just because Micky was a mate of mine. We shared the cell with a guy called Alex. He had spiky hair and he was very thin, but his special claim to fame was the fact that he was a really good portrait artist. He would draw pictures from photographs for other cons and also for some of the screws, and he would get paid in tobacco. We were always happy to get some burn into the cell, because with that we could buy whatever we wanted, including drugs. Aside from that, we survived on institutional food, letters from home, one visit a month, and a few luxuries from the money they gave us as a weekly allowance.

Every night in the cell Micky Burns would tell us stories. He made my first few weeks on the main prison bearable, because he was a real character. He seemed to cope well, and that helped me to think I would be able to deal with my sentence.

Eventually I was allocated for transfer to Preston, a Category 'B' prison. I was put in the sweat-box and taken from Strangeways to Preston. You can't sit down in a sweat-box; you can only crouch in them. There is a central corridor and there are cubicles on either side. There is a little window of smoked glass and you can see out of it, but people can't see in.

I could tell that the atmosphere at Preston was more laid back from the moment I arrived; even the reception area felt different. In Strangeways, just before the riots kicked off, things were very intense. There was even a different atmosphere between the remand side of the prison and the main side, where people were doing bird. There was more tension between the cons and the screws. That tension would simmer away for some years to come until the infamous Strangeways riots in April 1990, when part of the prison was destroyed, over 200 inmates and officers were injured and one prisoner was killed.

From that intensity we came to Preston. Some of the screws weren't wearing hats and their sleeves were rolled up; it was all much more casual.

I was sat in a room with all the other lads who had come from Strangeways, and one of screws said to us, 'Right, lads, you're not in Strangeways any more, you're in Preston now. Just relax, get your head down, and do your bird.'

I was really surprised by this different attitude. They put me in a reception cell in the basement for a few days, and then I went on to one of the main wings, still on closed visits.

Eventually I got friendly with a guy called Coops from Longsight and moved into a cell with him. Coops was a decent guy; he was in for burglary. His girlfriend came to visit him and sometimes she would be able to bring some draw in for him. He used to share it with me. I was missing Lisa and I was missing the drugs that she used to bring in. I was hoping that soon I would be back on open visits so that I could start to get my drug supply again. I tattooed Lisa's name on my hands because I was missing her. I did it with a needle, some water-paints and some cotton. I did 'Lisa' on my hands and 'Angie' on my mate's arm, because that was his girl-friend's name.

In Preston you can work in one of the workshops if you want. I had a job for a few weeks but it didn't last. I couldn't handle it. I tried sewing mail-bags, but because I couldn't use a sewing-machine I 'graduated' from that job to stencilling the writing onto the mail-bag. Brad, my mate from Liverpool, showed me how to do it. I would get an aluminium stencil, put that over the mail-bag, dip a shoe-brush in black ink, and then run the brush over the top of the stencil, leaving whatever lettering the stencil created – for example, '£500 in silver', or some-thing like that.

So that brought in some extra money, but I could not stand working, so I stopped that and stayed in my cell, banged up for twenty-three hours each day. I used to do exercises, and then I got into cleaning the cell. I polished the floor, and I managed to get some plants to make the place look more homely. The cell became my pride and joy.

It wasn't easy to get plants in prison, but I managed to. I got friendly with the cleaner on our landing, an old guy called Ron who was doing life. He'd done most of his time in Wakefield, a Category 'A' prison, and now he was finishing off the last few years of his sentence in Preston. Ron had brought some plants with him from Wakefield, so I got them from him in exchange for some tobacco; I even managed to get a set of oil paints from him too.

Everyday items that people take for granted become precious commodities in prison. I would always try to be careful with what I had so that it would last as long as possible. So, for example, if I got a match from somewhere, I would use a pin to split it in half – that way I'd get two uses out of a single match.

We wanted a nice cell, the best cell on the landing, and we were competing with some of the other lads to have the best 'pad'. We would polish the floors, and hang some abstract paintings that I had done on the wall. I used the back of a cupboard to paint on. I painted the keys of an electronic keyboard with the name 'Brian Eno' on it and an arrow pointing upwards, symbolic of getting high.

There was a mixed-race guy called Carl Bennett who I had known on the out. He used to work the door of a nightclub in Manchester. He was also a regular in the Reno in Moss Side, a well-known late-night haunt on the old 'front' near to where the Harp Lager brewery used to be.

Carl had been in Strangeways with me and had been transferred to Preston at the same time as me. He was on another wing but I would see him each day when we went out onto the exercise yard. We would usually sit by the wall and chat; we became good friends.

Carl had a lot of respect from the other lads; he was hard as nails but he was also really calm and placid. He'd had a fight when he was younger and someone had hit him with a broken beer-glass, and he still had the scar. He was broad with a slight pigeon chest.

Carl was a very cool guy; he wasn't a person who expressed his feelings, but he did think. I could see him thinking sometimes, and often it would be to do with what was happening outside. He had a lot of contacts outside and a lot of respect.

Every day, just before exercise, I would shout out of my window to him: 'Carl, are you coming out on the yard?'

Sometimes he would come out but at other times he didn't; if he didn't come out, neither would I. We would go out in the yard and walk around and then we would sit under the tree there and chat about things.

One day we were out on the exercise yard and we sat down, and I could see that Carl was struggling to tell me something.

'What's the matter, mate?' I said, and he showed me a letter he had received. Carl couldn't read or write, so he didn't know what it said.

'Will you read that for me?' he said.

I took the letter and looked at the envelope. It was from his wife. It turned out that it was a 'Dear John' from her, saying she didn't want to know any more.

'It's from your missus,' I said.

'Yes, I know.' He seemed to be staring out into space as if he knew what was coming.

'I'm really sorry, mate.' I was struggling to find the words to tell him what this letter said. 'I'm afraid she says that she's leaving you.'

He was silent for a moment and then he said, 'I knew it; I knew that's what it was about.' He was calm but you could see he was really angry. I knew the guy who was going with his wife; he was supposed to be his mate.

I felt privileged that he had asked me but sad that his wife had done the dirty, and he was going to be out in a few months! Carl was a genuine guy, he was a real friend; but like many of us, he had a habit to feed, and he had his fingers in all kinds of pies, including burglary.

I used to look forward to getting letters from Lisa. She would put her perfume on them and I would smell it and be reminded of her. She would write some of the letter in code, telling me about things that were going on outside, usually to do with drugs.

I used to press my jeans under my bed in a big valentine's card. We were all in blue now, as sentenced prisoners. We could go down to the laundry once a week to change our shirt and trousers. I found a pair of jeans that were bleached denim, and I kept them and washed them myself. I would press these jeans with this card; it still had the cover on it. The jeans had a perfect crease right down them and I would wear them for visits. I also had a shirt that was faded and it had a smaller collar. It may sound crazy now, but these things were important because they allowed me to have some individuality.

I was on closed visits for a while and then, right out of the blue, I got an open visit. I didn't know I was getting one. I thought they had made a mistake. I was really excited, as I had not seen Lisa for months. When she came in I was touching her legs and kissing her, and I could smell her. It drove me mad; I'd only been able to see her through glass since I'd got nicked in Strangeways.

She had some drugs with her, and although there was just a small amount, she promised to give me more next time. As usual, she passed them to me by kissing. I was overjoyed – I felt like I had won the lottery! It was so good to see her, and good to have her bringing drugs in again.

She came in again and gave me a kiss and passed some more drugs over to me. We knew what we were doing. It was mainly draw that came in. I was off the heroin now because I had gone through withdrawal at Strangeways.

There was a prison officer called Babyface. He was a young guy, and really cocky. He was arrogant and we didn't like him. If ever there was trouble anywhere, if it went off, he would be in there first.

By contrast, we felt that Mr Parker had some respect for us, and so we had some respect for him. He was an older guy and he had nothing to prove; he was just doing a job. Sometimes he'd slip us a cigarette.

As my release date approached, I started to get a bit 'gate happy'; most cons get this as their release date approaches, and I was no exception. I couldn't wait to get out. I made arrangements to meet up with Carl, who was due out a few weeks after me. The day I was released, I walked through the gates and Lisa was there to meet me.

I was free again.

Chapter 8

Hearing the Voices

It was great to be out. Life on the outside seemed really fast. This was because in prison everything is slow, so when you get out and look at the cars passing by, and people walking – all the normal hustle and bustle of life – it all seems really fast. But it felt good. Lisa came to meet me and I had my discharge grant in my pocket: £68.

Lisa and I took the train back to Manchester and then caught a taxi to William Kent Crescent in Hulme. Lisa had brought some draw with her, so we skinned up walking to the train station and had a joint while we waited for the train to come. When I got home I was able to relieve two sources of tension: first, we made love for the first time in months, and then we went out and scored some whizz. It was great to be back!

To celebrate the fact that I had just been released from prison, I suggested to Lisa that we have a bit of a bender. And so we did.

I went to my doctors and picked up my regular prescription; even though I'd been inside for nearly eleven months, the doctor still gave me my Valium, DF 118 and temazepam. We also asked for some 'Red and Greys', which are prescribed to seriously obese people to help them lose weight. This is a tablet form of amphetamine, and they are very strong. We went back to the flat, and that was the start of a nine-month-long drugs marathon.

I soon discovered that while I'd been away, a few problems had arisen that I needed to deal with. First of all, the electricity had been cut off yet again, and Lisa had been getting by with just candles. I had no idea that she had been living like this.

We put up with this for a few days and then I said to Lisa, 'This is no good; we need to find another place to live.'

I was taking amphetamines, and after three days without sleep, I went walking round the Bull Rings to find another flat. I found one further down the row, where the workmen had just refurbished the place. It had a new kitchen, and looked like it could be the ideal home for us. I kicked in the door and found that the electricity was on, and that decided it for me. I changed the locks and we moved in there.

The next day we went to Moss Side council and asked them if it was possible to move in. They made a few enquiries and found out that the place was ready for new tenants; they didn't know we had already moved in the day before. We signed on the dotted line and the flat was ours. Not many people wanted housing on the Bull Rings; that's why they were happy to sign the place over to us. There were also lots of people squatting in the Crescents and they wanted to stop that happening as well. If we rented the place from them, they would get the housing benefit. So they gave us the keys and it was ours.

Over the following weeks, we went about making the place our home; we covered the windows with plywood and painted the outside of it black and white. A lot of people we knew on the Crescents used plywood on their windows; it helped to secure the flat and make the place more private, and it also meant that we could have the half-lit atmosphere that we liked.

We decorated our home with modern colours and bought some bits of new furniture. While I was still off my head, I started to do quite a lot of work on the place – we wanted it to be nice. I spent my time putting up a partition, painting and making the place different, while Lisa was busy making it spotless.

This was 1986, and what would become the 'Madchester' scene was just kicking off. 'Madchester' was known for its music – indie rock mixed with dance – the clubs where that music was played, and the style of dress that went with it – baggy jeans and casual tie-dyed tops.

Meanwhile 'house' music had just arrived from America and the whole scene was about to explode. 'House' is a kind of repetitious electronic music that is made with machines; it was a new sound. We started to hear this type of music on pirate radio stations and the likes of Stu Allen on Piccadilly Radio. Artists like Farley Jackmaster Funk, Frankie Knuckles, Steve 'Silk' Hurley, Marshall Jefferson and Derek May were invading the airways. These guys were making superb music using electronic equipment; they were using sequencers, drum machines, synthesizers, samplers and various effects to create a distinctive sound.

Up until this point I had loved listening to different types of music – in fact music had been a big part of my life since I was a teenager – but now all I wanted to do was to make music. I couldn't read music, but I could learn how to programme machines; so I decided to build a home studio. I started by building my own speakers, and I wanted them to be awesome. I didn't have much in the way of raw material, so I broke into quite a few of the empty flats around the block and took the kitchen worktops out; I used these to make the speakers. I bought two massive 250-watt bass units and four Piezo tweeters from Maplin – two for each speaker. I made the cabinets deep, to give the sound some more bass; they were about five feet high, two feet wide and two and a half feet deep, and I lined the inside with loft insulation.

I went to a second-hand shop in Manchester called Johnny Roadhouse's – they specialized in music equipment – and I bought a separate amp and two tape-decks; later I got a reel-to-reel. I started by recording stuff off the radio and mixing it together using the reel-to-reel and the two tape-decks. I then bought a self-assembly drum machine, again from Maplin. I got it home and got out my soldering iron and sat there working out the diagram and putting it together. It took me a long time, but I managed it in the end. After a while I got some more money together and bought a Roland TR808 drum machine and a Roland SH101 analogue synthesizer, both of which were classic house-music instruments. As time went on, it became quite rare for me to venture out of the flat. I did a load of speed, stayed indoors and lost a lot of weight; all I did was sit in the corner mixing music. It wasn't enough just to listen to the music or to go to clubs and dance to it; I wanted to make it. House music was my life! The people I started to hang around with had the same interests as me.

There was a black guy called Kermit who lived in one of the other Crescents. He had short hair and he dressed well; he had a drum machine, and like me, he was heavily into amphetamines. We would chat and listen to samples of the drum patterns that we had created.

From my point of view, everything was going well; really well. We were picking up our regular prescriptions, and by now I was getting my methadone script again; I'd been on methadone for years. We were also buying various types of slimming tablets from other people on a regular basis. I would score whizz and heroin when I wanted to, I had Lisa with me, and I could work on my music night and day. In fact the music was on all the time, and I mean all the time, twenty-four hours a day. For nine months I didn't sleep. I sat in the corner of the room making things with my soldering iron, assembling various kits from Maplin to add to my collection of electronic instruments. When Lisa was asleep I would turn the music down slightly, and just carry on with what I was doing. I was getting thinner and I was pale. Lisa would make me some food, but I wouldn't eat it because I was so off my face and caught up with the music. I would top up on the amphetamine, and I was happy.

Then the voices started.

They came right out of the blue one night – no particular reason, they just started: aggressive, vicious-sounding voices, coming from everywhere. They sounded as if they were coming from outside my head:

'You b******, you f****** c*** ...' and so on. Swearing at me and cursing at me. I was horrified. Lisa was with me when it started, and I turned to her:

'Lisa, can you hear those voices?'

'What voices?' she said.

'Can you hear those voices?' I said again.

'No, I can't,' she said.

In my fear I got angry. 'Don't you tell me you can't hear those voices! Don't you tell me you can't hear them. They're there, they're everywhere!'

'Barry,' she said, 'they're not there – it's all in your head.'

'Don't you tell me they're in my head! You're with them, aren't you! You're all against me.'

I sat in the dim light of our flat, panicking as the voices found their way into our home and into my head. I thought they were coming from other flats; I thought maybe someone nearby had it in for me.

The worst of it was, they didn't stop, ever, night or day. Day after day the voices were there: 'You b******, you f***, you ...'

It wasn't just the language, it was the way the words were spoken, the vicious hatred in the voices. And I could hear them everywhere; even when I flushed the toilet, the voices came through the water in the flush. I was convinced it was someone, or some people, from within the Crescents, doing this to me.

There were some lads who used to stay in a flat across the walkway on the corner; they did a bit of shoplifting, and I thought they were looking out of their windows and shouting at me. I was even convinced that the people who lived above us were watching me through the cracks where the walls met the ceiling.

One morning, in the early hours, I thought I could hear voices from one of the flats where these lads lived, and I said to Lisa, 'Can you hear those voices? It's those lads from across the way.'

'It can't be them – they're not there any more,' she said.

I didn't believe her. I turned the music right down and listened intently. I could still hear the voices. I said again to Lisa, 'Listen, can't you hear them now?'

She looked me in the eye and said, 'Barry, there's nobody there.'

Right, that's it! I thought. I was furious. I put my trainers on and picked up the pick-axe handle that I kept by the door, and I rushed out of the flat. This was a major event for me – I hardly ever went out. I walked up to the top floor and across the walkway in the middle of the night, shouting my head off; and I climbed onto the banister that ran along the side of their flat.

I stood on the banister, five storeys up, at the side of the window of this flat where I thought these voices were coming from. I shouted into the flat, and then swung the pick-axe handle against the glass of the window, as hard as I could. The glass shattered under the force of the blow, and I looked in, full of anger, expecting to see them there. The flat was empty. I'd been convinced there was someone there, but Lisa was right, of course – they had gone.

I went back to our flat, still fuming, and told Lisa there was no one there.

'I told you,' she said. But I didn't believe her; I thought that they had just managed to slip out before I arrived.

I'd made so much noise that quite a few lights went on and people came out to have a look at what was going on. No one phoned the police, of course; no one ever did on the Crescents – not just for a bit of disturbance.

I was so frightened that I decided to stop taking the whizz. I thought that maybe the drug was doing this to me, and if I stopped whizzing the voices would stop too. By now I hadn't slept for nine months. I hoped that the voices would go away, but they didn't – they were still there, spitting their venomous curses at me. Then I started to get a feeling in my stomach, like a knot of constant fear. I didn't know what was going on, I was petrified. In the past, if I'd had a bad LSD trip, then I knew that after a day or two it would be okay. This was different, though, because the voices just would not stop.

There was a guy who lived on the top floor, called Simon; he was mixed race and he had green eyes. One day he knocked on my door. We got quite friendly and we smoked a bit of draw together. He came by one day, and we were chatting. I told him all about the voices I was hearing, and I found out he was into Buddhism and the occult. When I visited him in his flat I could see that he had a Buddhist shrine and I knew he was into a bit of black magic as well.

That was enough to feed my paranoia. In my bathroom there was an air-vent that led up to all the flats above and below ours, including Simon's flat. Sometimes when I went into the bathroom, I thought I could hear Simon shouting down through his vent at me.

I said to Lisa, 'I'm sure I can hear Simon's voice. He's shouting down at me from his flat. Can you hear him?'

She said, 'No.'

A few months passed, and then I became convinced that I had been cursed. I'd been to Simon's flat and I had seen all his occult stuff.

I said to Lisa, 'It's that Simon, he's cursed me!'

It didn't help my state of mind when there was a knock on the door one day, and I opened it to see Simon, dressed as a policeman. That completely freaked me out; up until this point he had always worn tracksuits and trainers.

'What's all this, man?' I said, indicating the uniform.

'What's what?'

'All this uniform and stuff! You're not a real copper, are you?' I couldn't believe it.

'Yes, I'm a policeman,' he said, smiling.

Well, anyway, I invited him in. He wasn't interested in nicking me for the drugs, but he knew I caused a lot of hassle on the block because of my music. He didn't mention this at all; he just sat down in his uniform and chilled out. I could smell the nick on him. He smelt like a copper. My head was totally wrecked. I sat there chatting with him, thinking about all the things we may have talked about in the past, wondering if I'd told him anything that he could get me arrested for.

And then I was thinking, *This guy's been coming in my gaff for weeks and he's Old Bill – and he even smoked a spliff with me!* That really did freak me out.

One day someone knocked on the door, and when Lisa answered it there was no one there. From that day on, I noticed that someone was knocking at the door and running away, or posting things through the door; I was convinced it was Simon.

Meanwhile the voices carried on relentlessly; in the end I said to Lisa, 'This is no good. My head's mashed; I need to go and see Dr Khain.'

Then Carl Bennett, my mate from Preston Prison, came to see me. At the time he was the person I respected more than anyone else. He came by and knocked at the door one morning, about 2 a.m. We skinned up and had a draw and we started chatting.

'Carl, I'm scared, mate. I'm hearing voices. There's people after me out there.'

'What do you mean?' he said, dead cool. 'What voices?'

'Can you not hear those voices?' I said.

'What's he on about?' he said to Lisa, who was with us.

'I tried to tell him, Carl,' she said, 'but he won't listen to me.'

Now Carl knew that Lisa thought the world of me. He knew she wouldn't lie, and so he must have made his mind up then that there was something going on in my head.

He turned to me. 'Just come with me,' he said. I trusted Carl, so we walked out of the flat and through the Crescents in Hulme. It was between two and three in the morning, and we went out into the streets of Moss Side.

'What can you hear now?' he said.

There were some bits of music here and there, but that was it – and for me, of course, there were also the voices.

'Carl, I can hear voices 24/7,' I said.

'Barry, there's nothing there. What have you got to be scared of?'

'It's those voices, Carl. Can you not hear them?'

'There's no voices there, mate. It's all in your head,' he said.

And while I didn't believe Lisa, I did believe Carl.

Well, I thought, *if Carl says it's all in my head, it must be all in my head*. I believed him – he was my mate.

This was one of the things that convinced me that I really did need some medical help. I went back to Dr Khain. It was the only time I went to see him for a genuine reason. Even as I was walking to the surgery, I could still hear the voices, hammering away at me. He said that I needed to be admitted to Cheadle Royal Psychiatric Hospital, immediately.

So with Lisa at my side, I got a taxi and headed for the hospital. I remember driving up the motorway, and it was raining, and the water was splashing up on the wheels. In the sound of the rain hitting the wheel-arches I could hear the voices cursing and swearing at me.

We came off the motorway and travelled down the A34 onto Wilmslow Road, then up to the hospital. There was a sign, 'Cheadle Royal Hospital', and two big stone gate-posts, with a stone gate-house called the 'Lodge' on the left. Ahead of us was a long, straight road that led down to the main building. On each side of the road were green fields and rows of trees. It was like driving through the grounds of a stately home.

On the right-hand side some park benches were scattered around for patients to sit on, and at the bottom of the road was an imposing three-storey Victorian Gothic building. The windowpanes were reinforced with a latticework of metal. The main door was in the middle of the central building, with wings stretching out on either side.

After going through the central admin block, I was taken to the wing on the left, or the 'Hollies Unit', as it was known.

My stomach was still in a knot and the voices followed me over the threshold and into the building. This felt worse than admission to Preston, or even Strangeways.

The voices, they're following me, I thought. *It's not just in the Bull Rings or in Hulme – they've followed me here.*

Cheadle is one of the nicest areas of Greater Manchester, but for me, Cheadle Royal Hospital was a dark place. I was entering the lowest point of my life. For the first time, everything was out of my control. I had to live with the clenched fear in my stomach and the voices in my head.

After admission, I was put into my room on the Hollies Unit, and this was my home for the next five weeks. I remember lying on the bed for the first time. The voices were so intense. I was scared, petrified and hopeless; and the worst of it all was that they weren't going away. Some time later one of the medical staff came to talk to me. He introduced himself as Dr Trevor, he took me into a separate room and then interviewed me, asking all kinds of questions. He filmed the interview to help with research into this kind of psychosis. He asked me where I heard the voices and what they were saying to me. I answered all of his questions honestly.

'This is not usual,' he said. 'Normally, when people hear voices it's a form of schizophrenia. But most people with this illness hear voices from inside their head. In your case it's voices from outside your head.'

He diagnosed me as having amphetamine psychosis. I had made myself ill through using too much amphetamine; my condition was so bad that it was impacting on my perception of the external world around me.

They put me on Stelazine, which is a drug used to treat schizophrenia. I also got some mild sleeping tablets, but they didn't work. I stopped taking all the other gear I was used to. Lisa came to see me every night; unlike prison, she didn't bring me any drugs. I actually didn't want any at that time because I was so worried and preoccupied by the constant, 24/7, evil, loud, aggressive voices.

One of the other guys on my unit was a schizophrenic black guy called Justin. He was only 22 or 23, and he had been in mental hospitals most of his adult life. He had uncombed, spiky, afro hair and he used to stare at people while chewing and rolling his tongue. One night Lisa was visiting me, and we were sitting in the lounge round a coffee-table. Justin was there and he stared at Lisa, like he stared at everyone. She looked over at him and said, 'What are you looking at?'

At this time he had a broken arm in plaster, and after she'd spoken he got up, came over to her and smacked her in the face with this plaster cast. Her face started to swell up immediately.

When I saw this I jumped out of the chair and started fighting with Justin. We were on the floor giving each other a good beating when the male nurses piled in and split us up. We were immediately put into two different rooms.

Lisa had a big black eye, and I wanted to get my revenge. I couldn't believe that he had hit Lisa. When I was a kid my dad used to say to me, 'Real men don't hit women.' This was a no-no in my book. It's something I had never done. And here I was, in this psychiatric hospital, and this almost complete stranger had smacked my woman right in front of me. I was angry. The nurses sat me down and had a chat with me to calm me down. They said that they didn't want any trouble on the ward. I realized that if I caused trouble they would ask me to leave, and I didn't want that; I wanted to stay because I wanted the voices to go. From then on Justin and I kept our distance, but there was tension between us.

Meanwhile I got friendly with a guy called Dennis who also used to hear voices. He was in his fifties and he was having electric-shock treatment. He would sit in his chair in the unit, rocking backwards and forwards most of the day.

I got on well with Dennis. He smoked like a chimney, but it was good to meet someone else who was hearing voices too. I went out for a walk one afternoon with Dennis and a couple of the other guys, and we visited one of the local shops. We must have looked like something out of the film, *One Flew Over the Cuckoo's Nest*.

There was a lady in the hospital called Betty; I don't know what she was in for, but she had been in for months and she really was insane; she had no teeth left. Betty was quite a character who kept the staff busy on the Hollies Unit. I remember one afternoon, just lying in my bed, in a room with ten other beds that were supposed to be male only – and in walks Betty!

It turned out that she regularly visited one of the other guys in our room. Neither the nurses nor the hospital authorities knew anything about this. He was diagonally opposite me, and she would come in, go over to him, pull the curtain round his bed and then have sex with him! She did this quite a few times; it was a strange and disturbing thing to witness, especially whilst the voices were still going on in my head. The fear I felt made me scared about going home. I still thought there were people after me in Hulme.

Then, out of the blue, my mam came to visit me at the hospital. I think Lisa must have told my brother Kevin where I was, and he'd told my mam. Over the years I had maintained some contact with Kevin. It might have been years in between us speaking, but he was always there. He hated the life I was living, but I was still his brother. He had an old J4 van that he used for work; it was full of paint and dust-sheets. He used it to bring my mam up to see me.

I was sat there, looking drawn, and my stomach was hurting. It must have been hard for her to see me in this state; I could see the worry on her face. It had been years since she had seen me. I'm sure she was just glad to see that I was alive, but she still had to come to terms with the fact that her youngest son was an addict in a mental hospital.

The treatment had made no impact on my condition, although they continued to give me Stelazine, and I would be on that for years to come. Stelazine does have side-effects; my eyesight was impaired, so I could see clouds in front of my eyes and the colours were really sharp.

With my lack of progress, it became clear that there wasn't much more they could do for me. The doctor came to see me one day. 'We are going to discharge you,' he said.

'I don't want to be discharged! I can still hear voices. I can't go home!' I was very fearful of what I would be returning to.

'I'm sorry, but there's nothing more we can do for you here.'

'What do you mean?'

'We will refer you to an out-patients' unit near your home. You can still be treated there.'

I pleaded with them, but it didn't matter; they discharged me and sent me home, basically in the same state that I'd been in when I'd arrived, weeks before.

I went back to the flat after I was discharged, and within two days I had a note from my doctor to take to the Housing Department, saying that I'd had a mental breakdown and that I needed to move out of our present home on the Crescents to a different place, out of Hulme, because of my health. I took this note to the council and asked them to sort it out as soon as possible.

Within a week we were offered a flat in North Manchester, on a council estate there. Straight away we got a bus and went to look around the place. It was great. It was in a tower block, but out in the sticks – just what I needed. It was like living in the countryside compared to Hulme.

But the voices came with me.

Chapter 9

Out in the Sticks

We hired a large Transit box-van to carry all our belongings, and we moved to the suburbs of north Manchester. The move was very helpful for me, and when we moved into our new flat we set about making the place feel like home. In the lounge we painted the lower half of the wall pale blue and the top half white. Then, using the same pale-blue colour, I painted an arrow on the wall, pointing upwards from the intersection of the two colours into the white. We painted the woodwork light grey and the doors black. I added my own distinctive mark to the doors by painting a line from the door-handle up to the opposite corner; everything above this diagonal line was painted and formed a triangle of grey on the door.

We put up some bamboo blinds and put in our low furniture; we'd already created this by sawing the legs off our tables and chairs. We had a table under the window near the door to the kitchen, and some bean-bags on the floor. I set up my studio equipment; we had the two big speakers that we brought with us, and we put one in each corner of the room to get the best possible stereo effect. Then we got some plants and put these down by the speakers.

We wanted to create a chilled-out and relaxed atmosphere like we had always had in our previous homes, so we put in some low lights and a flickering lightbulb attached to a small table; and we played lots of music. We had a parasol, and we placed a low-lit light behind it; and then we put a spotlight on the wall, highlighting our Bob Marley flag. The flag had the Rasta colours, Bob Marley's face and the word 'freedom' on it.

We soon got to know a few people and we had quite a bit of a social life going on; people would drop by and see us, maybe smoke a bit of draw and take a bit of whizz and have a chat. When we had friends round we would sit on the floor; the room would be full of smoke from the draw we were having. Nobody knew us; we were over from Moss Side and I didn't have any history with any of our new neighbours. In a way that helped, because I could see that there was no reason for anyone to be after me. I even started going out a bit more.

In time I began to believe that the voices were in my head and that my only option was to learn to live with them. The way that I used to deal with them was to talk back to them inside my head. On the outside I looked okay, but on the inside my head was in turmoil. The only other person on the new housing estate who knew about the voices was Lisa.

An older guy called Mickey would come round to see us. He'd recently had a nervous breakdown. He was an ex-alcoholic and had knocked about with some heavy people when he was younger. He had moved up from Ancoats and had moved in with a sensible woman who was good for him. She had a job and she kept an eye on him. He had managed to stay off the drink for a while when we knew him. He still used to smoke draw and he liked to come over to our flat to relax. He had a seventies-style Kevin Keegan perm, a neat beard and a gold earring. He smelt of roll-ups, but he was always clean and smart.

I also got friendly with a guy called Norman. He was a keyboard player, and he was also into electronic music. He had a mate with a computer that was loaded with music software; they would sometimes come round to the flat and plug their equipment into my mixer, and we would smoke a few spliffs and just make music together.

This was the late eighties, and Acid House was just becoming popular. I managed to purchase a Roland TB303 from A1 Music in Manchester to add to my studio, and this enabled me to create the distinctive sound for this type of music. I knew a music producer in Prestwich and he helped me learn how to programme it. I would go to his house and spend some time with him in his bedroom studio. With a bit of practice I managed to create some pretty good Acid House music. For me this was it: I just wanted to make music. I wasn't interested in making money, just the music itself. On one occasion I went up to Affleck's Palace in the centre of Manchester and put up a few posters offering my services, but nothing came of it.

While we were living in north Manchester we started to dabble a bit with 'crack', an extremely addictive derivative of cocaine. It gave an unparalleled degree of pleasure, but only for a short time. So you had to take some more to stay high, and the come-down afterwards was absolutely terrible. I'm so glad I didn't really get too involved with crack; a lot of our associates in Moss Side started to use it in a big way, and it completely destroyed them. Most of the time I stuck with my old favourite: heroin.

There was one time when I was so desperate to get stoned that I found some prescription medicine and drank all of it. I thought there might be something in the medicine that would help me get stoned. I think it was cough medicine! I got palpitations, I was sweating, and my breathing became irregular. I collapsed on the floor in the bathroom. I thought I was dying.

I was getting on with life the best I could, allowing for my psychosis. I was still using drugs, but not to the extent that I had been before my breakdown. I'd been living in the new place about a year, but it was only a matter of time before I got into trouble again.

One evening we bumped into an older guy who lived on the estate called Brian. We would see Brian at the doctor's when we were picking up our scripts, and from time to time we would chat to him. He was in his early forties and lived alone in a flat on the estate; he had a very drawn face, hobnail boots, short hair at the sides and a ponytail. Brian was a classic old-time alcoholic and drug user; he wasn't fussy about what he took. We had just scored, so we asked him if he wanted to come up later that night for an hour or two and spend some time with us. He was obviously lonely and we felt sorry for him; we thought we were doing him a favour.

So Brian came up that evening and he sat in one of the chairs, and in the corner was all the music-making equipment which we had brought from Hulme. Brian and I chatted, and he seemed interested in the music equipment. I turned everything on and started to explain how it worked, and Lisa offered him a sandwich and a drink. We didn't think he ate particularly well, and we wanted to help him out. Then he asked for the bathroom, so I gave him directions and he got up and went through while Lisa was still in the kitchen and I was sitting in the corner playing with my home studio.

He came back a few minutes later and sat down in the chair again, and I was still playing in the corner. Lisa came in with the sandwich and put it on the table, and I started to talk to him again, and he just lifted his hand and shook it slightly. I then noticed that he was wearing my watch! This watch had been given to me by a guy I had known in Hulme. This guy was into 'kiting' cheques – using stolen cheques to obtain cash and goods – and he also used knocked-off credit cards. When I'd been released from prison he had given me the watch as a 'welcome back' present. So he was one of my mates, and this watch meant something to me; it had sentimental value as well as being a really nice watch.

I used to leave it on the dressing-table in the bedroom; so that meant that Brian had gone into our room, seen the watch, and just nicked it. I looked at the watch, there on his wrist, just as he was reaching for the sandwich.

'Hey, that's my watch!' I said indignantly.

'That's not your watch,' said Brian.

'That's my f****** watch!' I said, louder this time, and I grabbed his hand and looked at the watch – and it was mine. I could tell without any doubt whatsoever, firstly because of the make, but also because the watch had a small scratch on the glass face.

'You've nicked my f****** watch!' I shouted.

'It's not your watch, it's mine!' he replied, but I could see that he was afraid, and that he was lying.

So then I lost it; I went absolutely mad. I had a proper riot-stick, about twenty-four inches long, that I kept next to one of my speakers, together with some of the flick-knives and lock-knives that I had collected. They were out on display on the top of a small table that was under the Bob Marley flag on the wall. I picked up the stick and I started to lay into him.

I never went looking for trouble, but on this occasion I was so angry that I whacked him quite a few times around the head and body, and he was squealing and I was shouting at him. I just carried on hitting him until eventually Lisa stopped me, shouting at me that I was going to kill him. I could not cope with the abuse of hospitality – it really offended me.

It seemed a long time before I stopped; but eventually I did, and Brian limped out of the place with blood running down his face onto the carpets. Within seconds the police came; someone in the block had heard Brian's squealing and called the police. Apparently they had a few phone calls, including, eventually, one from Brian. I'm not surprised, because he was making a lot of noise.

Normally I would have denied everything, but because I was so indignant I told them all about it. I thought they would be on my side. I told them that we had invited him into the flat for a sandwich, then he had the cheek to pretend to go to the toilet and go into my bedroom and steal my watch! The copper told me to calm down, and agreed with me that it was an absolute imposition that Brian should abuse our hospitality by trying to steal my watch. Unfortunately he followed it up by telling me that he had to charge me because I had given Brian a good beating.

So I was back in the police cells for a night or two, and they charged me with ABH and let me out on bail. I came home and word had got around that I'd half killed someone. I became a well-known person almost overnight.

My friend Mickey came round after hearing what had gone on, and I told him the story and when I was due in court. When the court date arrived, Brian never turned up. There was no witness and no proof, so they adjourned the case and issued a subpoena against Brian, requiring him to come to court. The CID even went round to see him. A new date for the trial was fixed, but again Brian was nowhere to be seen. I always wondered why Brian never turned up. Who knows? What I did know was that, without Brian there was no case, subpoena or no subpoena, and so I got off.

Meanwhile Lisa and I continued with our lives out in the sticks. We were doing the drugs, doing our stuff, but by this time things had changed between us, and we began to drift apart. We had been together for nearly ten years and we had stuck with each other through thick and thin. I was now about 28 and she was 39, and we were always together; but my feelings towards her were changing.

At the same time I was beginning to make some connection with my parents again. My dad went along with this for my mother's sake. He was still very hurt and quite angry with me, but my mother was worried. I'd only spoken to her a few times in seven years, and she had seen what I had looked like at Cheadle Royal. The relationship wasn't particularly strong. They never came to see us and we hardly ever went to see them, but at least we were talking to each other.

Lisa and I got to the stage where we didn't have much to talk about. In the past the main thing that we had in common was our hedonistic urban lifestyle, fuelled by extreme drug use. This was the glue that held us together, but now somehow it had gone.

I used to lie on the floor in our flat, near the fire, and look up at her sitting on the chair, and think of all that we had been through; it seemed impossible that we would split up. But I knew that I didn't think of her in the same way as I used to, so what was the solution? Should we stay together, just for old times' sake? To be honest, I think she was thinking the same thing. We were both adults and we knew each other really well; I think we both knew that it was coming to an end. We didn't argue or shout about it; we just agreed that it was time to move on. I stayed for a few more weeks and then we both went to the local Housing Department, so that I could sign over the flat into her name.

After that I left the flat. I had my own car and I just took my own clothes, and that was all. I had sold most of the musical equipment because I had made a decision that I was going to focus on DJ-ing; all that I kept was my small mixer and my two turntables. I left the speakers behind because they were too big and I had nowhere to put them.

I later found out that Lisa sold what was left of the musical equipment. She even sold the speakers to a dealer who lived in the block. She had no trouble selling them because they were well made and they sounded great.

Meanwhile Brian vanished; I never saw him again.

I decided I needed to earn a bit of money, so I applied for a taxi licence, got my taxi badge, and got a job as a private-hire driver. I worked for a firm near the centre of Manchester. It was a steady business and it kept me going and brought in the money I needed to keep my addiction going.

This job helped me get back into the routine of work. It also helped restore my relationship with my parents; they could see that I was trying to get myself sorted out. On the surface, things were looking okay, but underneath I was still an addict.

One Friday night, I'd just scored some heroin; and I could feel that it was really strong. I was driving up a main road and I started to 'nod' (the junky term for when your eyes close and your head nods down, because of the effects of heroin). My car veered to the right and into a brick wall. It was nearly a write-off.

On another occasion, about the same time, I was driving down the motorway while on heroin, and I was 'nodding'. I kept shaking my head to keep my eyes open. I was in the outside lane going really fast, and then all I remember is being woken up as the car ran into the metal barrier in the middle of the road and scraped down it for about a hundred metres, making a huge noise. The driver's side of the car was a mess.

There was one passenger who I used to pick up and take to work some days. We would have a chat in the cab in the morning while I drove her into Blackley; she had recently divorced, and over a period of time I discovered that she liked me, and I liked her. Eventually we decided to have an evening together. Tania was a good woman; she had her own house and she didn't do drugs; she was sensible and hard-working, and she did her best for her kids. She and I got on really well and eventually, after a few more dates, she asked me to move in with her.

I accepted the offer, and I settled into her life of family and work. At the beginning everything was great between us. We would go out in the evening, go out for meals, and do the things that normal couples did. This was all new to me; I had never done this before, and I really appreciated Tania and the relationship we had. Tania always looked good and she was great to be with, and I thought the world of her. But always at the back of my mind I was thinking, *How long is this going to last?*

I was taking methadone every day, which helped keep the monkey off my back – that is, it kept me free from withdrawal symptoms – and I was using amphetamines just to help me function. I was smoking draw, I was frequently using heroin and from time to time I was taking other drugs as well, including ecstasy. Tania knew nothing about this; she had no idea I was into drugs. Everything was okay; even her kids were happy to start with because they could see that their mam was happy to have someone again; like her, they didn't know that I was taking drugs.

After a while I noticed that there was a little bit of friction between me and her daughters. At this stage I was still into music: I was DJ-ing and practising a lot. Tania would be out at work in the day, and I would work on the taxis during the night. When I got home I would sleep for a few hours, then get up, go to Vinyl Exchange, a record shop in Manchester, buy a load of new twelve-inch records, and then come home and practise while everybody was out. Then I would take the mix tapes that I had done in the day out with me in the evening and listen to them while I was driving my taxi. I always had house music playing in my car. Sometimes at weekends, after I had finished work, I would then go to a rave for a couple of hours before I came home.

With hindsight, I have to say that I did not treat Tania very well; the drugs made me selfish, as they always had done. We were happy together, and this could have been a brilliant long-term relationship if it hadn't been for me. After an okay start, things began to go wrong. I always hid my gear in the car, never in the house, but I think Tania's daughters began to suspect that I was taking drugs of some kind, and it fuelled their resentment at my presence in the house.

I was continuing with my drug habit, and trying to do so without the rest of them knowing. I would go into the bathroom and have a shower and a shave before I went to work, and then I'd be on the toilet injecting amphetamine. There were a couple of moments when I thought I was going to get found out. I would be in the toilet for a long while, and they would bang on the door asking me what I was doing. The problem is, heroin and methadone make you constipated, and so I'd be on the toilet either injecting or trying to go to the toilet, so I'd take ages.

One day I was working on the DJ-ing and, right out of the blue, I found that I had mastered the art of mixing properly. It sounds like something that should be easy to do, but to do it well requires a lot of practice and dedication, to get it in time and in key. I also discovered that I could mix different types of music, for example opera and 'house'. I was really over the moon about this; I couldn't wait to tell Tania.

When she got in from work I didn't say 'Hello' or 'How are you?' or anything like that. I just said, 'Guess what!'

'What?'

'I can mix!' I thought this was the biggest news in ages, but clearly she didn't.

'So what?' she replied. She didn't have the same love for house music as I did; and no doubt she was tired and beginning to think about what the kids where going to have for tea.

'What do you mean, "So what"?' I said indignantly. 'I'm going to be a famous DJ; this is what I am going to do with the rest of my life.'

'Get real,' she said, weary of my typically selfish attitude. Of course, now I don't blame her at all. She had come in after a hard day's work to find me fiddling around with my DJ gear and getting excited about mixing. But at the time I was angry that she hadn't recognized what I thought was a very important achievement.

Anyway, after that it all kicked off and we had a blazing row. It wasn't just the thing about mixing, of course – we had been working up to this for months. And during the course of the row the whole drugs thing came out; she told me that she had suspected for some time, and that it couldn't continue – she had her kids to think about.

That was the final straw for me. I didn't feel like I belonged there, and so I wasn't going to stay. I knew the kids wanted me to go, and things really weren't working for anyone. Tania was a sensible, hard-working woman who was trying to do the best for her kids; and I was in a world of my own. We had had some good times during our three years together, but Tania and the children deserved better than me. They didn't need someone like me around.

When all the arguing had been done, I grabbed my Technics SL1200 deck, my small monitor speakers and my Aiwa amplifier, piled them together, and then headed outside and placed them in the boot of my car. Then as she watched, I stomped back into the house, grabbed my clothes and threw them into the car as well. I didn't argue any more, or go back for anything else; I just got into my car and drove away.

Chapter 10

Naked and Nicked

I didn't work that night.

Everything I owned was in the back of my car; everything that I thought I needed. I had my decks and my records and some clothes – and that was it. I'd just grabbed it all, and I was gone.

I knew that it was over between us. We'd had a few difficult moments, but this was the final straw. I had realized that when she found out I was taking drugs, this would be the end of the relationship. There was no way we could ever get back together.

Now I had nowhere to stay and nowhere to sleep; so I drove into the centre of Manchester. I always ended up going into Manchester town centre when I didn't know where to go; it was like home for me. That evening I drove around the town, thinking about Tania and the kids, and the fact that they now knew for sure about the drugs. I thought about some of the things we had said to each other in the heat of the moment; and then all of a sudden I sensed God.

I can't really describe it any other way. I was suddenly aware of a supernatural presence, as if I was being led. I felt like someone was standing behind me, watching over my shoulder. This was nothing to do with me hearing voices. I was used to that and I'd lived with it for some years by now. This was more to do with a realization that God was there and that, in some mysterious way, he was leading me. It was the most amazing thing.

I knew that I had at last mastered the art of mixing; so I began to think about making a living out of DJ-ing and about producing my own record. This was unusual for me, because the thought of making money out of music was the last thing on my mind; but this thought was with me as I drove around the centre of town.

That night I had nowhere to sleep, so I went to one of the car parks in Manchester town centre and slept in the back of my car, across the seat. The next day, when I woke up, I still felt that sense of calling; I was convinced that God was leading me. My mind was still preoccupied with the previous night's thoughts about DJ-ing and producing my own record.

I went to a local garage and bought a Bic razor, some shaving soap, a toothbrush and some toothpaste; then I went into the toilet and got cleaned up. I came out and my mind was fixed – not on getting myself accommodation but on getting the extra equipment I needed to make a 'demo' track.

I bought a copy of *Loot* magazine and I sat in my car and started to look for the things that I would need to get this recording together. I needed some quality monitor speakers, a good amp, a Teac 4-track recorder, and a top-of-the-range Akia Sampler. I went in to A1 Music and Johnny Roadhouse's to see what they had in stock and to find out the cost of this equipment. I worked out that if I could sell my car for £3,000, this would cover it.

I drove to the Northern Quarter of Manchester. There was a professional recording studio there, hidden away in one of the back streets. I had recently read an article in a music-making magazine about some of the dance music artists who had used this place. When I got there the door was open and so I walked in, and there was a black guy sitting behind a big mixing desk. I peeped through the door and he saw me.

'Come in,' he said.

I walked in and looked around the place. It was amazing; an Aladdin's cave for someone like me.

'What can we do for you?' he asked.

I told him that I had been involved with making music for some time in my home studio and that now I thought I was ready to produce a record. I told him that I had my decks in the boot of my car and that I had a few ideas of how the track would sound. While we were chatting, my attention was caught by some of his equipment, and we then got into a conversation about it. He could see that I knew what I was talking about.

We chatted for about half an hour, and at the end of it he said I could use this studio, but it would cost. He told me the hourly rate, and it was expensive; but then, this place had everything I'd ever need to lay down a track. I left there feeling encouraged, realizing that this was the guy who had produced and remixed some top dance tunes in the early 1990s. I thought I was in the right place.

All that day I drove round town, visiting music shops, making phone calls to people about ads in *Loot*, doing my sums, and trying to work out the best approach: get the extra equipment I needed or use the studio?

At about 1 o'clock in the morning I was still driving around Manchester city centre with my head in the clouds – and then something crazy happened.

My dad has a phrase that he uses to express his opinion that something is unlikely to come to pass. He will say something like, 'I'll show my backside if [such and such] happens!'

So I was driving around and I felt that something was going on, that I was on a journey and I had a purpose. I felt really focused.

As I was coming to some traffic lights I suddenly said to myself, 'If those lights turn red before I get to them, I'm going to show my backside on Buxton market!'

And as I got to the lights they turned red.

'Right,' I said to myself, 'I'm going to show my backside on Buxton market.' I was a man of my word. I had said it, so I was going to do it.

Now Buxton was thirty-five miles away; so I started to drive towards it, and I was thinking, *I'm meant to be going this way. I'm meant to be driving down this road.*

And eventually I picked up the road signs which pointed me towards Buxton, and as I was driving along I was convinced that God was leading me this way. As I drove on, I had an overwhelming sense that I was being led to a particular place for a particular purpose.

I continued to drive towards Buxton, and even the road signs seemed to be part of this plan. If there was sign with a number of towns written on it, the name 'Buxton' seemed to be brighter than the others. I felt like God was leading me to Buxton. This was where he wanted me to be.

By this time I was driving my taxi while disqualified. I'd recently been banned from driving for a year because I had accumulated over twelve points. That didn't worry me because I'd applied for a duplicate licence before I got banned, so I could keep on driving and keep working illegally.

I arrived in Buxton at about 2 o'clock in the morning. I drove through the town slowly until I found the marketplace. I got out of the car, and I had this real sense of excitement – *this was it!*

And I pulled down my pants and said, 'Right, I said I would show my backside on Buxton market, and there it is!'

Now Buxton is a beautiful market town in Derbyshire; and of course, at 2 o'clock in the morning there was no one around at all; probably a good thing!

I got back into my car and pulled round the corner, and that's when I heard the siren.

Oh no! I thought. *I'm driving without a licence. I'm going to get nicked!*

I pulled in, and the police car stopped behind me. One of the police officers got out of the car and came to the driver's-side window. I wound down the window and looked up, trying to maintain my cool.

'Good evening, Officer,' I said in all innocence. 'Have I done something wrong?'

'No sir,' he said, 'just a routine check. Can you show me your licence, please?'

So I showed him my duplicate licence.

'What are you doing here then?' he asked.

'I just dropped a passenger off down the road.'

He looked at the licence again.

'Okay, thank you, Mr Woodward,' he said, and gave it back to me.

I don't think he bothered to check with anyone; he certainly didn't use his radio or anything; and off he went.

So I breathed a sigh of relief, and set off again, driving around Buxton. Now Buxton is an affluent town: big houses, big gardens, it's really a beautiful place. And I was driving round thinking, *That's it, I've shown my backside, and God has brought me here for a purpose.*

I realized I needed somewhere to stay. I had some money with me; I could pay for a room okay, and so I started to drive around and look for accommodation. I knocked on some hotel doors, but it was now 2.30 in the morning and no one wanted to take me in. I asked at a few places, and they all told me there was no space. I felt a bit like Joseph and Mary looking for a room with Mary pregnant, and there being no room for them anywhere.

I got back into my car and continued to drive. After a while I pulled up at the roadside because I'd seen a path that led round the side of this huge stone house. This could be it, I thought. This could be the place where I'm meant to stay.

I got out of my car and walked round to the back of the house. The building was flanked by a metal fire-escape stretching to the top floor. I looked up and decided that I needed to climb up there. I had no intention of breaking in; burglary was never my thing; I just felt that I needed to climb the stairs.

I climbed up the fire-escape, still thinking that this was the place where God wanted me to be. When I got to the top I looked in through the window and tried to open the fire-escape door, but it was locked. I climbed back down as quietly as I could, almost tip-toeing, and walked back to my car.

I got back in the car and started to drive again, and then I saw another road sign. Again, this one seemed to be illuminated and it stood out from the rest, and so I followed it to what I now know to be the Pavilion Gardens. The sign led me to a car park.

I stopped my car, opened the boot, and pulled out one of my boxes of records. I picked it up and then I walked down a narrow footpath and over a small bridge, and I could hear the gushing sound of the stream that ran underneath.

I ended up in a kids' play area. There was a little play-shed there and a climbing frame and there was broken bark on the ground. I put my records in the play-shed, thinking, *God's brought me here.* And so I started to shout, 'THANK YOU, GOD! THANK YOU, GOD!' at the top of my voice.

I looked around at the play equipment and I said to myself, 'Right, if I can walk round the top of this climbing-frame without touching the sides or falling, then everything is going to be okay.'

So I climbed onto the frame and wobbled my way round, avoiding the sides and trying to keep my balance – and I made it! I thought this was another sign.

'THANK YOU, GOD!' I shouted again. 'THANK YOU, GOD!' Again, I had an overwhelming sense that God had called me there.

It was now about three in the morning, and it was a beautiful night. The sky was clear and there was a full moon. I was thinking, *God is with me. There is a God. He's called me.*

So I left my records in the play-shed and walked down to the stream, and I stood at the side of the bank for a couple of minutes, thinking, *God's brought me here.*

And then as I looked at the stream I thought, *I need to walk across this stream. I need to do this.*

So I took all my clothes off. I stood there completely naked, and then I walked across the stream towards the other side, and I was thinking, *I am being cleaned by doing this, by walking across this stream. This is great!*

When I got to the other side and walked up the riverbank, a row of buildings appeared. *This is where God has called me to be,* I thought. *This is where I need to be.*

I now know that these buildings, and their grounds, were the famous Pavilion Gardens in Buxton. Owned by the council, they were built in the Victorian era, at a time of economic boom for the town. The building now serves as a venue for conferences and artistic events – and I was wandering round there at three in the morning, completely naked, thanking God for calling me to that very place.

I approached one of the buildings and I looked into a window, and in my imagination I thought I saw a recording studio in this building – all of the equipment I would need. I thought, *This could be the place where I'm meant to make my record.*

I walked around for a while, and then I started to knock on a door. Not once or twice but several times over.

'God's called me here. Can you let me in, please!' I shouted. 'I'm going to make a record.'

Eventually a woman came to the door. She looked out at me, and I said, 'Let me in! God's called me here.'

I was standing there completely naked.

Unsurprisingly, she didn't let me in. Instead of opening the door she left it firmly closed, and moved away out of my sight. I now realize that she went to phone the police.

I walked further along and came to a building that housed a swimming-pool. I later found out this was the Buxton Spa Baths. The door was locked, and I ended up sitting with my back to the glass on a ledge that ran along the outside of a large window. Looking in, I could see light reflecting on the water of the baths.

A few weeks before all this, I'd had a vivid dream. In my dream I fell through some water, and while I was in this water I saw every colour you could imagine – colours never seen before, vibrant and sharp – reds, greens, purples, yellows. And as I fell into this water I felt so clean and fresh. I felt as if I had been made pure. As I fell into the water, I fell through, and I came out of the other end, and I was all clean and I felt new and excited and full of life. The dream had been so powerful that I'd woken up straight afterwards; it had been on my mind ever since. Remembering the dream now, I thought to myself, *Maybe this is me falling into the water. Maybe I am going to fall through the water in these baths and it will be the dream coming true.*

As I was thinking this, in the distance I saw the flickering blue light of a police car making its way slowly up one of the narrow paths that ran through the gardens. There was no siren, just the flash of the blue light.

It was the police again! I ran back down the bank towards the stream, the police car still in the distance, and I waded back through the stream in the direction I had come from, and on this side I could see a stone outhouse. I ran up to this small building and crouched behind it, keeping still and trying to hold my breath.

By this time the police had arrived and I could see the blue lights reflecting all around me. I stood there listening and I heard the car doors open and close. I peeped round the corner and they were only fifty metres away, and they were walking towards the outhouse. I moved round the outside wall with my back to it so that as they walked round it, I walked round the opposite side. I tried to work out what I should do; and I thought, *Oh no, I'm going to get nicked; they're going to get me.*

So I ran down to a different part of the stream; it looked quite deep. I stood on the edge with my back to the river and I was holding my nose to stop the water getting up it. And the dream came back to me again: *This is it, I am going to fall into the water and feel clean and see the bright colours and have that wonderful experience that I dreamed about!*

By this time the police were just five to ten metres away; there was a man and a woman. The policewoman spoke to me: 'Come here, love,' she said. 'Are you all right? Are you cold?' She was holding a blanket. I had seen this kind of blanket before; it's standard issue for a police cell – rough wool and beige coloured. The river was behind me and I was thinking, I am going to fall back into the water and *I am going to go all the way through, like in the dream. This is it!*

So I closed my eyes and fell back. I thought I was going to plunge into this big pool of water, but it was only about a foot deep! As I jumped back, the water splashed all over me. I stumbled but managed to stay up straight; and I just stood there in this water. It was absolutely freezing!

I ran to the bank and the policeman crouched down and gave me his hand to help pull me out; the police-woman passed me the blanket.

'Come here, love,' she said. 'Put this around you. What are you doing here?'

'God's called me here,' I said.

'Come with me, love,' she said. She put me in the car. I sat there shivering, and they were both really nice to me. I can see now that they had taken pity on me.

I ended up in the cells at Buxton Police Station and I spent the weekend there. Like the coppers who had picked me up, the desk sergeant thought it was all quite funny. Officers would come and see me and ask what I'd been up to. I would tell them all the same story: 'God's called me here.'

'Oh, all right, mate,' they laughed.

They were great with me, really. They came every time I called them when I wanted a light for a smoke. They called me 'Barry' and not just 'Woodward'.

The police picked up the car, the records, my clothes; everything. They put the car into the compound. The police made some enquiries and discovered that I was driving while disqualified, so I got charged with that, and I also got charged with a 'non-reportable offence' or indecent exposure – which is fair enough, since I was wandering round the Pavilion Gardens at three in the morning, stark naked!

I had a long list of previous convictions, and now I had been caught driving without a licence; so yet again I was remanded in custody. I moved from Buxton police station to Chesterfield holding cells. While commuting to the court, I told everyone – the staff and other remand prisoners – 'God's called me.'

All during this time I had a kind of peace about things. I thought I had everything I needed. I thought that when I was out again I would be able to go and make my record, and nothing was going to get in my way. I had my decks, I had the right combination of records to mix and sample, and I had my car to sell to get some extra money. The thing with Tania was over. I knew that when I got out I'd go back to DJ-ing. I had it all worked out.

This episode seems as vivid to me now as the day it happened, back in 1992; and as crazy as it seems, I still believe that God was in this somewhere. He needed to get my attention, and in the middle of the mess that was going on in my life at the time, he got it. It wasn't the bit about being a DJ or producing a record; that was just me going off on one. But he was there in it all. Through the haze of the drugs and the voices, I began to have a sudden awareness that God was there and that in some way he was directing me. I began to say then what I am still able to say today – that God was calling me.

Chapter 11

No Fixed Abode

The magistrates put me on remand in Leicester prison. It was the same routine as before – I went through reception and then I was taken on to the hospital wing. They had heard about my arrest in Buxton and they were concerned with my mental health. This time I was placed in a cell on my own rather than on a ward with others.

I was still convinced that God was calling me, and I told the screws this. I don't wonder at the fact that they put me in the hospital wing! I remember sitting in the room on the floor, legs crossed, wearing the white gown they had given me, and thinking: *God's called me, this is it. I'm going to spend some time in here and then I'm going to do the music; just like I've planned.*

At the time I still thought I would be able to get my car, my decks, and my other stuff back after I had been up in court. I was expecting to get bail; after all, they were only minor charges.

For the first few days they gave me some DF 118s to help with my withdrawals, so at least in that respect times had really changed since the early eighties. Then all you could hope for was a couple of aspirin and a long session of cold turkey. The tablets helped a bit but they certainly didn't take all the pains away. I was assessed by a doctor, and then eventually I was transferred to one of the main wings.

I got put in a cell with a guy called Pete. He was also on remand, for burglary. He really struggled with the fact that he was locked up. I think it was his first time inside. He was okay; we didn't get on that well but we managed.

After being inside a few weeks, I decided I wanted to have my hair cut; it was getting a bit long, and I always liked to keep it short and neat, in a crew-cut. So I found out when the prison barber, another prisoner, was working, and I went down to get it cut. I sat myself in the chair and he asked me what I wanted done.

'Number three, please, mate,' I said. That was my usual when I was on the out.

So he got out some hand-clippers and started to cut away. I could feel the clippers tugging at my hair; at times it was really hurting. He kept unscrewing the cutters and blowing on them and tapping them. He didn't look like he knew what he was doing. After he had done half of my head the clippers stopped working because they were so blunt. He went away for a few minutes, and then came back and said, 'I'm sorry, mate – the clippers are broke and I can't find any more!'

So I was sitting there with half of a number three and the rest of my hair uncut. 'What am I supposed to do?' I said. 'Walk around with half a haircut?'

'No,' he said, 'you can shave it all off. I can get you some extra Bic razors if you want.'

Well, I was furious, but I had no other choice. I told him what I thought of it as I snatched the extra razors from him and went back to my cell.

When I got there I took the small mirror down from the wall, went to the recess, filled my bowl up with water, brought it back to my cell and started to shave all my head. It took quite a long time but eventually I managed to get it all off. I'd wanted a number three, but ended up with a zero. I was completely bald! When I looked in the mirror I thought: *I look like Buddha! What am I going to do? I can't walk around like this.* But of course I had to.

When one of the screws opened my cell door to let me out for my tea, I could see some of the lads looking at me; they must have thought I'd really lost it. I'd told a few people that God had called me and this had got round, and now I'd shaved all my hair off. To be honest, some of the inmates were a bit wary of me – and one uncharacteristic burst of violence did nothing to help my reputation.

One morning, about two weeks later, I was coming out of my cell to slop out, and there was a guy in the next cell called Fred. He was a small, stocky guy in his late twenties and he was from Leeds. He had a real Yorkshire accent and a borstal dot tattoo on his face. I was gasping for a smoke, so I turned to him and said, 'Give us a smoke, mate.'

'I haven't got any smokes,' he replied.

Now, I knew this wasn't true, because Fred worked in the kitchens and it was one of the best-paid jobs in the prison. I knew he had been paid the day before so he was bound to have had some burn.

'You liar,' I said, 'you got paid yesterday!'

He said again, 'I haven't got any, mate!'

So I walked right up to him, eyeball to eyeball; and then I snapped my head forward and head-butted him, as hard as I could, right on his forehead. Next thing, we were laying into each other. I'd started on him just because he lied to me. It wasn't like it was a major thing; this happens all the time in the nick. If people didn't want to give you a smoke they would just say that they didn't have any. I used to say it!

Anyway, the alarm bells went off in the prison, and a load of screws came running down from the different landings to the first floor where we were fighting, and they separated us; as they pulled us apart each of us was accusing the other of starting the fight.

They dragged me off, and I was still struggling and swearing and kicking out. Four screws took me away to another part of the prison, then they put me in a strait-jacket. The straps were used to wrap my arms around my body, and then they tied my arms behind me, under-neath each other round my sides. They tied it tight, and all the time I was struggling and shouting.

After they'd put the straitjacket on me, they threw me in a padded cell and banged the door shut behind me. The cell was about two by two and a half metres in size. There was no furniture in there at all. The walls, the floor, and the door were overlaid with thick white padding. I lay on the floor and it was completely silent. I couldn't hear a thing – only my own heavy breathing, the rustle of the straitjacket, and the long straps flap-ping around. I couldn't go anywhere or move. Eventually I calmed down. I just lay there, thinking, *I don't believe this. What was that all about? I'm only in for driving while disqualified, and here I am, banged up in a padded cell!*

The prison officers kept coming to the spy-hole: 'Are you doin' all right in there, Woodward?'

'Yes, Boss, I'm doing fine. When can I get out?'

'When you've settled down.'

And so I waited.

Eventually, when they were sure that I had calmed down, they took me out of the padded cell and placed me in the block, pending a visit to see the Governor. I was cautioned and then taken back to the wing. I still don't know why I snapped on that guy; I was not by nature a violent person. When I got back I found that I now had a bit of respect because I'd had this fight with Fred. People were even more wary of me now.

Every day I went out onto the yard and I chose to spend time on my own. I knew quite a few of the lads, who I had met in other prisons, but I chose to keep myself to myself. Most people would walk around the yard in circles, anti-clockwise, and chat with each other, but I would just sit on the floor in the corner with my legs crossed, on my own. I would speak to some people occasionally, but I was mainly consumed with the fact that I still thought God had called me. This strong feeling had not changed; I still thought I had a calling from God and I was going to make a living out of DJ-ing as soon as I got out of prison.

There was a guy in a cell opposite me called Blacky. He was about six feet two with a short haircut, and he was a hard lad; he had his hand in plaster and a black eye. He used to walk around with just his light-blue tee-shirt on; the cons weren't supposed to do this. Usually you had to have your shirt on, but he didn't care. When I got back to the wing after being in the padded cell, he asked if I wanted to move in with him. I knew that he had just got out of the block for fighting, and he had quite a lot of contacts inside the prison because he was a local lad, so I said yes. That afternoon I asked one of the screws if I could move in with Blacky, then later he came back to my cell and told me to get all my belongings together because they were moving me across.

It was good to move in with Blacky. I think the fight had earned me his respect. That first night he got out some weed and rolled a spliff. He had loads of it. All we did was sit in the cell and smoke draw. This was good news for me because I didn't have anyone coming to visit me, and so I didn't have my own access to any drugs.

After eight weeks on remand I was taken back to the High Peaks Magistrates' Court, found guilty, and sentenced. I got banned from driving again and received a fine. I left the court-room in an expectant mood. I thought that everything would still be okay; after all, I had my car and my decks and my records. The problem was, I had nowhere to live. I knew that I couldn't live at Tania's, but I wanted to know where my car was and my DJ-ing equipment, so I gave her a call from the pay-phone outside the court-room. She asked how I was doing and I said I was fine. I asked how she and the children were doing, and then asked her where my car was and my DJ-ing stuff. I knew that my car had been impounded by the police in Buxton but I didn't know what they had done with it.

'Your dad got a bus to Buxton and then drove it back,' she said.

At first I couldn't understand why he had got involved in the first place, but then Tania told me that the police had contacted him.

'Why did my dad go and get it?' I asked her.

'He said you owed him some money, so he picked up the car and then sold it.'

There was a bit of a pause; it was clear that she wasn't enjoying this conversation any more than I was.

'He's sold my car?' I asked.

'Yes,' she said, in a quiet voice.

I couldn't believe it; this was my own car that I used for taxiing – and my dad had sold it. But then I thought, *Well, it's true – I did owe him some money, so now we're straight.*

'Okay, Tania, my dad's sold my car. So where is my DJ-ing gear?'

There was a long pause; I suppose I should have known what she was going to say.

'Where's my decks and my mixer?' I asked.

'I've sold them,' she said finally. 'I needed the money.' Somehow everything that had been in the car had ended up at Tania's house.

I was just shocked; this equipment was my pride and joy, and she knew that.

'How much did you get for them?' I asked.

'£300.'

I couldn't believe it. She had practically given them away! Still, I could see why she might have done that; she'd needed the money.

'So where are my records?' I asked.

There was another silence, and then she said, 'I've sold them too.'

I was devastated. *No!* I thought. *Not my records. I can replace my decks but I can't replace the records.*

It had taken me years to get this collection together; many of those records were hard to come by. I couldn't just go out and buy the same ones again; some were probably irreplaceable now.

I still remained calm and positive. I remembered all that I had put her through, and I thought to myself, *I don't blame her, she's a good woman.*

I told her not to worry, that I could get some more. I said I would pop by to pick up my clothes that had been left in the back of my car, and then I put the phone down.

I travelled back to Manchester on the train and then I called in to see Tania; but while I was there her oldest daughter came in from school and got upset, and said that she didn't want me there, and that she would move out if I came back. I didn't blame her for reacting like this.

It was clear that I could not stay with Tania any more. It was definitely over.

I left her house and made some phone calls, and my only option was a hostel. I ended up at the Salvation Army hostel on James Street in Salford.

Initially the idea of staying in a hostel didn't seem that good, but I had no choice. I had 'no fixed abode', nowhere to stay. I knew that if I booked into a hostel, I could put my name down with the local housing department and wait to get my own place. I'd decided early on that I wasn't going to take any old place; I was going to use the hostel as a stepping-stone into somewhere that I really liked. So while I was in the hostel I applied to different housing associations and the council, and when I got the forms back I was able to pinpoint different areas around Salford where I wanted to live. One of them was near where my mam lived. There were some housing association properties there.

At the hostel most of the residents were older than me. Some of them had been in there for years and they were content with living this lifestyle. They had a roof over their heads, they had three meals a day and it was warm. Most of them would get their benefits and blow them in a few days on drink, and then they would wait to get their next giro and blow that on drink too. They lived for their next giro.

Despite their situation and outlook on life, I still respected some of them. There was one old guy called Billy, or 'Tobacco Bill', as he was known. He had got this name because he used to sell cheap tobacco that had been brought in illegally from Europe. Billy was from Salford; he was about 76 with grey hair and a bent back, and his breathing was terrible. He smoked like a trooper and he drank a lot. I was very fond of Billy and I respected him. I used to go to his room at times and we'd chat about life and everything. We used to sit in the TV room together. He had a story to tell. He'd lived his life and now he was just waiting to die. But he wasn't going to go down miserable; he was happy and content, despite all his ailments. He had a woman friend who used to come and see him a few times a week. That was a highlight for him. Billy knew how to make the best of living in this sort of environment.

Staying in the hostel was a low point for me; I never thought that I would end up in a 'doss house'. I had had all these hopes and dreams, but for the first time I was beginning to think that it wasn't going to happen. Reality started to kick in, and the ideas that I had had soon ebbed away. I still had a sense of destiny, that God had called me, somewhere in the background, but the ideas about producing music and DJ-ing just weren't that important any more. I was more concerned about finding myself a home.

The James Street hostel was very basic but it was very clean. We each had our own room, with a sink. We had to be out by 8.30 a.m. to give the cleaners time to come in and sort out the rooms, but we could be back in at 1 p.m. The manager of the hostel at the time was a woman called Mrs Main. She was a very strong woman. She was small physically, but she didn't stand for any nonsense; she commanded some respect. I behaved myself, kept my head down and planned to get a decent place from the council or the housing association when something came up.

By this time I had started to drink alcohol again. While I was with Tania I had started to have a social drink, and now from time to time I would go into various pubs near the hostel and have a few pints, that's all. One of these was right next door on James Street; it was called The Jollies. The landlord was an Irish bloke called

Chris. Chris was a happy-go-lucky kind of guy who liked to have a bet, usually without his wife knowing, and he liked a drink. The Jollies was full of local Salford people and there were a few who were residents in the hostel. At times I used to go in there.

I'd been in the hostel for nine months, drinking a bit and still taking methadone, but not using heroin; during this time I had a number of offers from the council and various housing associations, but none of them were suitable. But then I was offered a one-bedroom flat not far from my family – so I took it.

Straight away my brother Kevin offered to decorate. I used to share a room with Kevin when I was kid. He was older than me. When we were growing up together we had had our moments, like most brothers do, but he didn't let this get in the way of his loyalty to me, his youngest brother.

I got a furniture grant. I got a second-hand cooker and everything else that I needed to make this place my home, and I got it looking good. I then moved out of the hostel and into my new flat, and life was beginning to look up for me again.

Chapter 12

One-Night Stand

The Jollies was a rough-and-ready pub, really down to earth, and there were all sorts of characters in there. Sometimes I used to just sit and people-watch. There was a guy who used to go in the pub called Disco Dave. Dave was a big bloke with a beer-gut; I guess he was in his mid forties. He wore jeans that were always slipping down, so he had a 'builder's bum' showing. He had longish, shoulder-length, black, straggly hair, he was always unshaven and he wore a lumberjack shirt. He was a big, grizzly-bear type of guy. Disco Dave did a variety of things to make ends meet; he owned his own disco equipment and did old-style DJ-ing – a total contrast to the Haçienda DJs.

There was another guy called Joe. Joe was a scrap man. He was small and bald, and in his fifties; he wore a flat cap to keep his head covered, and his clothes were always dirty. Each day he would go out with his hand push-cart and collect scrap from different parts of Salford. By dinner-time he had traded in his scrap, finished his work for the day, and he was sat in the pub with a pint in his hand.

I carried on visiting The Jollies after I'd got my flat, although maybe not as regularly as when I was in the hostel. One day I realized I hadn't been in for a while, so I decided to have a Saturday night there.

It was the same old Jollies: the jukebox was playing, and it was smoky and everybody was just having a good time. I'd had a few pints and I was just talking with some of the locals, just having a laugh, and then this young girl came in; I guess she was about 17 or 18. Now by this time I was 30, and I could see that she was much younger than me; so I took no more notice of her. But she kept looking over at me and smiling, and I was flattered. As the night moved on she continued to look interested in me, so we started to chat.

'All right, love,' I said. 'Do you want a drink?'

'Yes, please,' she said, so I got her a drink and she came and sat with me. We had quite a few drinks together and chatted, and I found out she was from Salford Precinct. At the end of the night I asked her if she wanted to come back to my place. She said yes, and we got a taxi. Now by this time I think we were both fairly drunk. I certainly wasn't thinking straight, and really the testosterone had taken over. Once we were in the flat I put on some music and then we started to kiss on the settee. It wasn't long before we'd moved into the bedroom. We got undressed, got into bed and ended up having sex. She was the first girl I had been with since I had split from Tania.

I woke up the next morning and saw her lying next to me, and I thought, *Oh no! What have I done? I slept with this girl without any protection. I don't know who she is; I can't even remember her name.*

When she woke up I tried to get her out of the flat as soon as possible.

'You're living here on your own,' she said. 'I could come and live with you and keep you company.'

That was the last thing I wanted. 'No, I'm fine, thanks,' I said. 'I like living by myself. Maybe I'll see you in the pub sometime, though.'

I was thinking about what had happened, and I wondered how many people she had actually slept with, and what diseases they might have had; and I started to worry. I got her a taxi home and was glad to see the back of her.

We'd had unprotected sex – no condom, nothing. I didn't even know anything about her, only what she had told me the night before.

Two weeks went by, and I was just going about my business. And then I started to feel a bit strange; my mouth was going dry, I felt weak and I lost some weight. Over the next few days this got worse and worse. I couldn't put this one-night stand out of my mind, I kept thinking about it, and about how much I had regretted it; and then the thought came to my mind: *I've caught something from her. Oh no! I've caught AIDS!*

I'd really talked myself into this, I was convinced. I went into The Jollies again that night, and I sat at the bar feeling absolutely awful, and all I was thinking was, *I'm going to die. I've got AIDS from that woman and I'm going to die.*

A friend came to talk to me, but I couldn't concentrate because I was so worried. That was the last time I ever went into The Jollies; the place had too many bad memories for me.

I went to the family doctor's where I used to go when I was a kid and I told them about how I was feeling and about having unprotected sex. They told me that it was too early to tell, but the symptoms that I had were not related to any sexually transmitted diseases. I was unconvinced, and I came out of the surgery and said to myself, *They don't know what they're talking about.*

I really thought that I was going to die. When I was a teenager AIDS wasn't around, so we never used condoms when we slept around. I had been in two steady relationships that had spanned thirteen years. Now times had changed and HIV and AIDS were in the news, but I didn't understand anything about this new disease. I was 100 per cent convinced that I had caught it and I was going to die. At that time no one could have told me any different. I didn't mention this to my family; I didn't want them to hear it. I didn't tell anyone. I just lived with the thought that I didn't have long to live.

I decided that if my time was up, I might as well go out with a bang. So I decided to get some drugs from a dealer in Salford that I knew. This was the start of another bender, only this time I wasn't celebrating being released from prison, I was trying to blank out the thought of dying. When I was high on drugs, it stopped me thinking about the problem. I started to buy a lot of amphetamine – in fact, I bought anything I could. I started to shoplift again to give me the money I needed to keep the drugs coming in. Only this time I was more reckless, taking chances, doing crazy things. I soon added another load of charges to my name, but I didn't care because I thought I was on my way out.

I had never before done drugs to self-destruct; I just did them because I enjoyed them and enjoyed being off my head, but now I thought, *If I am going to die, I am going to go out in style.*

I used to visit my parents from time to time. Often my mam would make my tea for me and even my relationship with my dad was getting better. It wasn't like it used to be when I was younger, before the drugs spoilt everything, but I think he was trying his best. The trouble was, I had this cloud hanging over everything: I thought I had AIDS and was going to die; and I could not bring myself to tell them.

I remember going to Mam and Dad's once, and I was sitting in the living-room with them, and I thought, *After*

*all the stuff I've put them through, now they're going to see
me die.*

My eyes filled up with tears, but I managed to hide
behind the paper I was reading. This happened a number of
times and I never felt I could talk to them about it. I didn't
want to hurt them even more than I already had done.

When you believe that you are not going to be around
long, it changes the way you think. I cut myself off from
some of the people that I was close to because I didn't
want to hurt them. I lost even more weight and I started
to lose my confidence. I had butterflies in my stomach. I
didn't want to go for a test at the hospital because if it
came back positive, then I would know for sure that I
had it. I would try to pretend that everything was going
to be okay, but I certainly wasn't fooling myself. I was
dying and no one could help me.

One night I couldn't sleep. I was tossing and turning
with worry. My mouth was dry and I felt really weak. I
really was desperate, so I threw off the duvet and knelt
down at the side of my bed. I clasped my hands together and looked up towards the sky and with my eyes
closed, I said, 'GOD, HELP ME!'

I had prayed crisis prayers before, when I was due in
court or being chased by the police; but this was more
sustained – not just a panic about that moment, but a cry
out to God for the future, for my life.

My physical and mental state began to deteriorate. I
could still hear the voices in my head, and that condition
was aggravated by the fact that there was a busy road
next to where I lived, and the noise of the cars blended
in with the vicious curses of the voices. Now on top of
that there was this AIDS thing, and I had to live with
that too. This went on for two years; I thought I was living the last months and weeks of my life, and I was waiting for the end to come.

One night I was watching the TV. Now usually, whenever anything came on the box about HIV or AIDS, I would just change channels; but on this night I was looking through the channels and stopped at one where they were talking about AIDS, and there was a panel of experts talking about this illness. I was about to turn the station over, and then one of them said, 'Well, AIDS takes a period of time to incubate.' And that made me pause. I left it on the channel for a few more minutes and listened to what they were saying, and I realized that if this was the case, I had more time to live than I had thought. I had believed that with all these symptoms, I'd be dead pretty soon.

These few comments on the TV actually gave me some sense of optimism, and I thought to myself, *If I go for a test, even if I am HIV positive, I could still have years to live.* So I decided to go to the clinic to find out for sure.

At this time I wasn't working and I wasn't doing any of the music; I was registered as long-term sick and was getting any benefits I could. I got a free bus and train pass; I was eligible for all of this because of my psychosis and addictions.

So I went for the test at Hope Hospital on referral from the doctor; and then I went back for the results. I remember sitting in the waiting-room; I felt like I was a condemned man, getting ready to be executed. My name came up and I walked in and sat down, then the nurse picked up her paperwork, looked at me and said, 'Mr Woodward, the tests have come back negative.'

I looked and her. 'What – you mean I haven't got HIV?' I said.

'No, Mr Woodward, you haven't got HIV.'

I was in total shock; I just stared at the nurse for a moment, and I couldn't quite believe what my ears had just told me. I walked out of the hospital like I was walking on air, and I thought to myself, *I'm not going to die, I'm NOT going to die, I haven't got AIDS!*

I got outside the hospital and all of the relief and emotion welled up inside me, and I shouted at the top of my voice, 'THANK YOU, GOD! THANK YOU, GOD!'

Even after that it still took a few days for the results to sink in, and I realized that I had been totally ignorant about AIDS. I'd been living like a condemned man for two years because I'd not had a clue about this syndrome. Perhaps I should have listened to the doctor in the first place. All this time, since my one-night stand, I'd never used other people's needles and I'd never let them use mine – for their protection more than anything else. Of course, that practice had also protected me from anything anyone else might have been carrying.

I had lost weight, my mouth felt like the bottom of a bird-cage and I had no confidence; but now I knew that it wasn't AIDS. For the first time in two years I had some hope for the future. I also found out I was clear of all of the other diseases that drug users get, like hepatitis. Some time after this, the doctors wrote to me to ask me to go in. They diagnosed the illness I did have and were able to cure me. My life returned to what was, for me, a normal state; and I thought things would be okay for me.

Then one night it all went wrong again.

It was the early hours of the morning, and I was asleep in the bedroom when I was woken up by a noise outside the window of my living-room. I lived on the first floor, set back above a shop, and I could hear someone on the flat roof of the shop, just outside my lounge window.

I came out of the bedroom and there was a bloke standing outside, staring at me; 'Open this f****** window!' he shouted.

My window was slightly open but locked. There was no way I was going to open my window to this guy, so I pulled it closed and locked it again. This guy saw what I had done, and he turned round and reached down to the top of the roof and grabbed a paving-stone that one of his mates had passed up to him, and he started banging it hard against the window. The glass smashed and scattered over the lounge carpet.

I watched all this happening and I was horrified; I couldn't cope with it. I was living with all this stuff going on in my life, and I had no confidence, and so I panicked. I managed to escape by going through the front door, which was on the other side of the flat from the lounge. I ran down the stairs, across the grass and away. I had nothing with me except the shorts, T-shirt and trainers that I had quickly put on. I waited in the cold of the early hours until I was sure that they would be gone. In the end it was about two hours, and then finally I came back to my flat and had a look around. There was blood all over the window where the intruders had cut themselves on the wire in the glass pane they had smashed. Once they'd got inside they had taken my stereo, my video and my TV. The place was a mess, and as a consequence, I was a mess.

I had a good idea who had done it; they knew that I had no phone and that I lived on my own; so in many ways I was vulnerable. The police did come and investigate it, but I didn't grass these guys up; it just wasn't something I'd do. I thought to myself, *I don't need this, I just want a quiet life. I'm off.*

The next day I got some of my clothes, put them in my Adidas bag, picked up my travel pass, and then got a bus into the centre of Manchester. Then I walked to Victoria train station. I thought, *This free pass will take me anywhere in the Greater Manchester area. Where can I go to get as far away from Salford as I can?*

I looked on the list of train stations and I saw Rochdale. I thought, *That will do.*

While I was waiting for the train to come, I made some phone calls and found out that there was a Salvation Army hostel in Rochdale. When I arrived at Rochdale train station, I asked for directions, and from there I walked through the town until I eventually found the hostel. They had some space and admitted me, so at least I had a roof over my head and I felt safe.

The hostel was similar to the one in Salford, but the rooms were a lot smaller and there were more residents. I didn't like the idea of staying in a hostel once again, but I had no other choice because I had nowhere to stay. Besides, I wasn't planning to be there long. As soon as I was booked in I got in touch with the housing associa-tion who owned my old flat in Salford, and I told them what had happened. They told me that they also had some flats in Rochdale and that I had enough points to have one; but there was none available yet. So I put my name down on the waiting list.

While I was in the hostel I kept myself to myself. I was still taking the methadone and still hearing voices; and I still had a constant fear in my stomach. This sense of fear was always with me, and the episode in Salford hadn't helped.

I was just biding my time, using the place as a stop-gap until I got an offer from the housing association. I was expecting to stay at the hostel until the housing association found somewhere for me, but things didn't turn out that way.

There was a young guy in the hostel called Mike from Oldham. He was only 18 years old and he was really cocky and full of himself. He was always ripping off the old guys. His feet stank so badly that you could smell them through his trainers. He had yellow teeth, black hair, and he would sit in the TV room with his feet up all the time. I didn't have much time for Mike. I used to watch the way he treated people and it used to wind me up. He thought he owned the place.

His room was on the other side of the hallway to mine, and one afternoon I was in my room, lying on my bed, just chilling out, and he was playing his music really loud with his door wide open, just to annoy everyone. And I thought to myself, *It's okay, I'll ignore him, I'll just ignore him.*

I lay there and all I could hear was this music, blaring out. In the end it was driving me mad, so I went over to his room.

'Turn that f****** music down!' I said.

As soon as I had gone he turned it up, just to annoy me. I lay there, and I tried not to let it bother me, but in the end I thought, *Who does he think he is? Does he think he runs the place?*

And something in me just snapped. I ran out of my room and into his room and grabbed hold of him and started to beat him up. As I laid into him, his stereo smashed on the floor and his room ended up in a right mess.

When I'd finished, I just went back to my room and closed the door, and I thought, *Wow, what was that all about? I've not kicked off like that for years.*

Meanwhile Mike went down to the office. He was holding his bleeding nose and he was covered in bruises and cuts, and he grassed me up to the management. So the next minute the manager came up and confronted me. I didn't deny it; I couldn't, really.

They made me pack my bags and then they kicked me out. They kept records of every resident at the hostel; and the manager wrote a note on my records: 'BARRY WOODWARD: NOT TO BE LET BACK IN, VIOLENT AND AGGRESSIVE.'

I got my things together and walked out of the hostel, trying to work out where I could go next. I found out that there was another hostel in Rochdale called Leopold Court. By now it was about 10 or 11 o'clock at night, but the staff there let me in and told me that they had a place for me. This was a council-run mixed hostel that had just been built. The rooms were really nice with their own en suite facilities; much more luxurious than the Salvation Army hostel.

I settled in at Leopold Court, again determined to keep my head down and keep out of trouble. A few weeks after I had arrived there I got a letter from the housing association; they said they had a flat available for me. I went and had a look at the place and it was brilliant – a really nice flat. It was just on the outskirts of Rochdale. So straight away I moved in. I had put some of my belongings from my other flat in storage in my mam's shed, so I hired a van and moved everything in.

I was living in a great location; it was the ground-floor flat of a two-storey block at the bottom of a cul-de-sac. I had a big living-room, a nice kitchen and a view overlooking a football field. Again my brother Kevin came up to help me decorate the place, and I made it my home.

I thought my life was beginning to come together again; but I didn't realize that something far bigger than anything I had ever experienced was about to make an impact on me. Things were about to change, big time.

Chapter 13

God Encounter

Now I had the chance for a new start. I was in a new place where nobody knew me and I had a new flat. I was still on benefits, as I had been for years, but I felt like this was a good time for me to settle down and just try to get on with life. I would visit the doctor to pick up my regular prescriptions, including my methadone, I'd go for a walk, and I'd take the bus into town. I had a regular routine, I felt settled. By this time the experience that I had had in Buxton was more or less forgotten; music was in my past and the thought of being called by God was just a faint memory. I didn't feel any sense of calling, I didn't want any sense of calling; I just wanted to survive and live some kind of normal life.

To give me some company, I went to a dogs' home in Manchester and bought a little Jack Russell, and I called her Kim. I would take her out for a walk every day to some hills behind a hospital called Birch Hill. This was a big trip out for me, a major part of my day. By this time the drugs had taken their toll; the bravado was gone, the ambition was gone. I didn't feel confident about myself, who I was, what I could achieve. My world had closed in and I was happy for that to happen.

On a Thursday I would go to the Post Office and cash my sick-book; then I'd walk across the road to the bus stop and get a bus into the centre of Rochdale and do a bit of shopping. This was a big day out for me. Apart from taking my dog for a walk and going shopping once a week, I would stay indoors; that was my life and I was content.

One particular Thursday, I'd cashed my book and got my money and I was on the bus, and at the first stop after I had got on, a guy boarded the bus with his wife, and he ended up sitting next to me because the bus was quite full. The bus carried on its way and this guy started talking to me.

Now usually when I was on a bus I wouldn't talk to anybody. I'd just look out of the window and day-dream, but this guy was really quite friendly.

'All right, mate,' he said, 'how you doing? This bus is a bit full today, isn't it?'

'Yes, it is,' I said; I was a bit surprised that he'd started talking to me.

'My name's John,' he said. 'Do you live round here?'

'Just up the road from here.' I was deliberately vague; I didn't want to tell him where I lived.

John was about five foot eight and in his mid thirties; he was a stocky guy and he wore glasses. He had tattoos on his hands, with a small borstal dot tattooed on his face, and he spoke in a local accent. I could see there was nothing pretentious about him; he was a really down-to-earth guy.

I told him my name, and we ended up chatting about music. It turned out that he was into soul and I said that I used to be into dance music. We chatted about our musical tastes until the bus arrived in Rochdale town centre.

I got off the bus first, and as I stepped off and started to walk, I thought, *He was all right, that guy; he was really genuine.*

Then I went on into town and did my shopping and came back home. During the rest of the day this encounter came to mind; I would think about John and I was intrigued.

He was all right, that bloke, I thought. *What is it that he's got that I've not got? He was really genuine.*

The following Sunday, I was walking up past Birch Hill Hospital, taking Kim for a walk on the hills behind there, as usual. It was just after midday, and I saw John coming down the road towards me, and this time he was out with his wife and kids. When our paths crossed, I said, 'Hello, how you doing, mate?'

'I'm doing all right.'

'Fancy seeing you here. Where have you been?' I asked him.

'Oh,' he said, 'I've been to church.'

As soon as he said that, I thought to myself, *What on earth does he go to church for? Church is for older people, church is for boring people. He doesn't look like a church-goer!*

I really was astonished. To me churches were empty old buildings that you might see one or two old ladies in on a Sunday. I didn't know what to say; I was a bit shocked, so I just said the first thing that came to my mind.

'Oh, that's cool, mate.' I doubt whether I sounded very genuine, but then I wasn't!

John continued chatting: 'The church meets every Sunday in the hospital grounds,' and he turned round and pointed in the direction of the hospital. 'It's really lively; they get people over from America sometimes, it's great. Why don't you come along sometime?'

I thought to myself, *No way, mate! You're not getting me in church – that's the last thing I need.*

But I wanted to be polite, so I said, 'No, you're all right, mate; I'm not into church, but thanks for asking.'

'Oh, all right, then. See you,' he said.

We said our goodbyes; he went on his way and I went on mine.

The next day I was again taking the dog for a walk up the same road to the same place, and as I was walking past the hospital I thought, *I wonder where this church is that John goes to.*

So I started looking for a church. I was expecting to see a big old building with a steeple and stained-glass windows; somewhere that looked like a church, or what I thought a church should look like. But I couldn't see anything that matched that description.

Again, the next day as I took the dog for her regular walk, I looked again for this church, and still I could not see anything – no spires, no steeples, no Gothic structures. It was just one of those things that bugged me a bit; it gave me something to think about while I was out.

On the Tuesday I had an appointment with my psychiatrist. I had been seeing psychiatrists on a regular basis for nine years, since my breakdown in 1986. I'd been living in my new flat for four weeks. Up until this point I had been travelling back to Manchester city centre to see my doctor, during which time my medical records were being transferred over to Rochdale. This was my first visit to my new psychiatrist and the appointment was at the hospital near where I walked the dog.

So I went into the hospital grounds and found the psychiatric unit. I went to the reception area, gave my name and then sat down; eventually my turn came and I was asked to go into one of the doctors' offices. When I walked in, there was this African guy sat there; his name was Dr Samuel Yangye. He had a nice suit on with a black polo-neck jumper; he had very neat hair and gold-rimmed glasses. He was in his early forties. He pulled out my medical records and then asked me some questions about my circumstances. I told him how I was feeling and he was still happy for me to continue to get my prescription. So from my point of view this was a successful visit to the doctor. *Great*, I thought, *I can still get all my prescription drugs, and I can also keep getting all my benefits.*

Again, the next day I took Kim for a walk, and again I looked in vain for this church that John said he went to. I had a good look around but there was nothing that looked even remotely like a church.

The next day was a Thursday, and I was at home in the morning when there was a knock on the door. I opened it and I saw a woman standing there. She was about five foot five, quite well built and in her fifties, with ginger hair, and she spoke with a very broad Rochdale accent.

'Are you all right, love? My name's Dot and I'm your next-door-but-one neighbour. I've seen you out with your dog. You're from Salford, aren't you? I know you've not got much stuff, and I've just got a new fridge, so I was wondering whether you wanted to have my old one.'

I was surprised at how much she had found out about me, and to this day I still don't know how she did it. I thought, *I've got a fridge already but I could sell one of them.*

So I said yes to the offer. We had a bit of a chat on the doorstep and then, just as she was about to walk away, I said to her, 'Dot, can you do me a favour?'

'Yes love, what is it?'

'On Sunday I was walking up Birch Road and I met a guy, and he said he goes to church somewhere in the hospital grounds. Do you know where that church is?'

'Oh yes!' she said. 'I know where that church is – I go to it. I'll come for you on Sunday morning and take you, if you want.'

I was so surprised by her comment that I just said, 'Oh, okay,' and even as I spoke the words I thought, *Oh no, what have I let myself in for? I don't go to church!*

It was true. I was 32 years old and I'd never gone to church as a child except for weddings and funerals. My family wasn't religious in any way. The only time I had gone to church as an adult was when I went to the chapel in Strangeways Prison, and that was so that I could get out of my cell for an extra hour on a Sunday. I had prayed a few crisis prayers in my time when I was desperate, but that was about all. Of course, I'd had some kind of experience a few years before where I felt like God was leading me to Buxton and that God had called me, but I still never prayed or went to church. In fact, it would never have occurred to me to connect experiencing God with going to church.

At this time I was actually getting into New Age stuff; I used to burn incense, I had a few crystals in my flat and had started reading books on meditation. I would sit in my bedroom on a cushion chanting a sentence to help clear my head and to help me focus while I meditated. That was my venture into spirituality at the time. Church was the last thing on my mind.

So Sunday morning came round, and true to her word, Dot called for me. I was a bit hesitant, but she had offered to call for me and pick me up and I didn't think going to church once would do me any real harm. We walked up Birch Road together and then she led me into the hospital grounds and then towards a brick building that had a wooden extension attached to it. There was a sign outside that said 'Doctors' Training Centre', and I thought, *This isn't a church! Where's she taking me? I thought we were going to church! Where is the vicar, and where are the bells, and the graveyard and all that?*

We walked through the door and into the foyer, and there were some kids playing there; and then we walked down the corridor and round the side into the wooden part of the building. We came into a room with a dark-blue carpet down on the floor, pale-blue walls, and a low ceiling. There were about fifty chairs out, and I could see an overhead projector standing on a table and a wooden pulpit. That's all. This wasn't what I was expecting. I thought this must be the church, but it didn't feel like a church building.

What am I doing here? I thought. But it was too late to back out. So Dot and I sat down and some of the people started coming up to me, saying, 'Are you all right? It's nice to see you. Where are you from?'

And I thought, *These guys don't even know me, so why are they so pleased to see me? Why are they being so nice?*

I sat down on the second row, with Dot beside me, feeling really uncomfortable. I was in a strange place with these people, and I knew that I couldn't just back out; I had to go through with this now I was here. There were people rehearsing some music at the front and other people were just arriving. People were chatting with each other; most of them obviously knew each other quite well. A few came over and talked to Dot, and then turned and said hello to me.

I'd never had so many people be nice to me in such a short space of time, never. It was a total culture shock to me and I didn't know what to do or what to say. And then, just as I was trying to get my bearings, there was a tap on my shoulder, and I turned round and there was John, the guy I had met on the bus!

'All right, mate,' he said. 'I didn't think you were coming.'

Neither did I, I thought. *This is really bizarre. What's going on here?*

So John sat down next to me on the opposite side to Dot. His wife and two children sat next him. I then told him that Dot had knocked on my door and I had asked her where the church was and that she had brought me. He was really excited about the fact that I was there, but I was still wondering what I was doing in church.

Then the leader of the church stood up at the front and stood behind the pulpit, and it seemed like he was putting his notes in order. I thought, *He must be getting ready to start.*

I was sat there expecting the meeting to begin, and just before the minister said his first words, someone walked in the door behind me and shouted in a loud voice:

'Hallelujah! Praise the Lord!'

I turned round to have a look, and it was my new psychiatrist! The same guy who I had had my first appointment with just a few days before was standing there, with his wife and kids; and they came and sat behind me.

I thought about the fact that I'd been in a completely new flat for just about four weeks; nobody knew me in this area apart from those who'd been in the hostels in another part of town. Then within about ten days, I had met three people – Dot, John and my psychiatrist – and they all went to this church. I tried to work it all out. Was it some conspiracy? Had they planned it so that they could get me to church? How did John know I would be in here? How did he get on the bus one stop after me? How did Dot move into her flat before I did? Now, I was still suffering from amphetamine psychosis, and so I was used to thinking this way – looking for a conspiracy, looking for some signs of collusion amongst imagined enemies. It had been with me since my time on the Bull Rings, and, even though it was much less intense, it was still with me that day when I arrived at church.

By now there were about forty people in the building, and I was still thinking that this was some kind of set-up. I was wondering how this had all happened, how between them they could have arranged it. I was still hearing voices at this time and that didn't help. I thought it was all pre-planned, but I didn't see how that could be.

Finally the meeting started and a guy with a guitar started singing. The songs were different; they weren't anything like the few hymns I could remember from my times in church. Then one guy started dancing a kind of Pentecostal two-step – and I was in culture shock! I'd never seen anything like it in my life before. The guy leading the church was dancing! This was really bizarre, and a far cry from the dancing in the Haçienda and the Acid House style that I was used to.

I was still reeling from all this alien stuff when Dot got a tambourine out of her bag in the middle of the first song and started to bang this thing on her hip. I couldn't believe it. I thought, *If my mates from Manchester could see me now, what would they think?*

I then looked over my shoulder and saw my psychiatrist. He was dancing around, and he seemed to be singing in a different language. It certainly wasn't English or his native tongue, and it seemed somehow different from any other language I'd ever heard; and I thought to myself, *This is my psychiatrist. If he's supposed to be treating me, what chance have I got?*

So I carried on feeling really uncomfortable, really out of place and disorientated, and I was looking around and most of them were going for it, singing and dancing; and John next to me was raising his hands and singing. It was bizarre: a big bloke like him with tattoos raising his hands in church. But although I was completely out of my comfort zone, there was something else, beyond all of the things I could see and hear; and I thought, *What am I doing here? What's happening? This is crazy, but there's something going on here.* In the midst of feeling uncomfortable, I could sense that there was something else; even though I was nervous, I was also intrigued.

So the singing stopped and then they had communion. They passed the bread and juice around, and I can't even remember whether I took it or not. Then the kids went out and then Alan Reeve, the church leader, stood up and started to deliver his message. I can't remember very much of what he said but at the end of it he said: 'If you believe in a God who can heal you, we will pray for you, because we believe in a God who can heal.'

It wasn't over the top, he didn't shout, and it wasn't hyped up. He asked for people to come forward who wanted prayer for healing; and I thought, *Well, I have some kind of belief in God.* From time to time I would think that there must be something out there, something a bit bigger than me. I remembered the experience that I'd had in Buxton. I'd certainly believed in God then.

So I thought to myself, *I'm going to the front. I need some prayer. What have I got to lose?*

So I stepped out of my seat and walked to the front of this little wooden prefab, and I was the only one stood there; I felt a right fool. I could feel everyone else's eyes staring at me; and then Alan came up to me and stood next to me and said, 'What can I pray for, for you?'

'Well,' I said, 'I'm addicted to methadone, I've been using heroin for fourteen years, I've got no confidence, and I've been hearing voices in my head for years.'

I was totally honest about the way that I was with him; I'd given up any idea of pretending by this time. He closed his eyes, and he put his hands on my head and he started to pray that God would heal me, that God would release me from the voices, and take away my addictions. And as he was praying, the guy who had been playing the guitar came over and stood with us, and he put his hand on my shoulder. His name was Howard.

And as Alan started to pray, I began to feel really hot, like fire rushing through my body from my feet up to my head. I had goose-bumps and the hairs on the back of my neck were standing up on end, and I knew that whatever this was, it wasn't anything to do with me being ill. Also, I knew that it wasn't some kind of withdrawal symptom because I'd had my methadone for the day. This was something completely different, completely new!

Then I started to cry, tears streaming down my face; and I was shocked at myself; I had not cried for years, I never cried. Then I started to shake, as Alan was still praying for all my needs. I was burning, there was an intense heat running all the way through my body, and I was also crying and shaking. And these two guys were praying over me, and then started to speak in a strange language similar to what my psychiatrist had been using, and I thought, *Wow, this guy is speaking in Hebrew. What kind of a church is this?*

Then Alan said, 'Amen,' and I knew enough to twig that this was the end of my prayer time.

I remember that when he was praying for me, I had my eyes closed, but it was as if I had my eyes open and I could see around me; there was a kind of brightness there. I stood there with my eyes closed and I was still shaking and crying, and then after a few minutes I walked back to my seat.

I knew that something had changed. I felt hot and there was a spring in my step; I knew that something had happened to me. It wasn't a long process, it was sudden and powerful. I sat down in bewilderment, totally gobsmacked. I had never expected this.

At the end of the meeting, while I was still trying to process everything and work out what had happened, John turned to me and said, 'That was God, mate.' He had a smile on his face. 'You've just met God!'

I don't think I gave him any kind of answer. I didn't really understand what he meant, but I was completely convinced that something had happened. I felt like I'd been knocked down by a bus, and I had got back up again; but somehow I was different!

'There's a meeting on tomorrow,' said John, 'at the Methodist church down the road. Noel Proctor's speaking. Do you want to come along?'

'Oh, I know Noel!' I said; 'he used to be the chaplain in Strangeways Prison.' I remembered the time he came to visit me in the block and give me an extra-strong mint, which he called an anti-swearing tablet.

But I wasn't sure about going to this meeting. I was still quite overwhelmed by what had just happened. So John said he could give me a call. So I gave him my home phone number, and then we left.

I walked home with Dot and I started to ask her some questions about what had happened to me. 'You know that guy who plays the guitar,' I said; 'he was praying in Hebrew!'

'Oh no, love,' she said, 'he was praying in tongues. It's a gift from God! It's a language that God gives us to pray in.'

I thought, *Wow, God can give you a new language to pray in!*

When I got home I said goodbye to Dot, walked into my house, and shut the door behind me. For the first time since I'd had this experience, I was on my own. I stood still and listened. I was expecting to hear the voices, as I had done for all these past years. I was getting ready to cope with this by talking back to them, as I had learnt to. But then I heard something I had not heard for years.

Total silence. Complete, total silence. No voices, no cursing and swearing, no foul language. The voices had totally gone! I had lived with the voices for nine solid years, but now they had gone. I had been prayed for, and the voices had gone!

I moved to a different room and stood still again and listened, but I could hear nothing. I went into the bathroom and flushed the toilet, because usually I could hear them in the water flushing round, but there was complete silence. No voices. Totally amazing!

Then I noticed that the sickening tension in my stomach, the sense of fear that had blighted my life for so long, had gone as well. For the first time in years there were no voices, and there was no fear in my stomach. This had to be God.

I walked into my bedroom, threw my jacket on the floor, and thought, *I've just had an encounter with God. That's what John was on about. He knew what had happened to me.*

I'd been taking street drugs for over fourteen years; I'd injected myself pretty much anywhere I could get a hit. I rolled my sleeves up and looked at the mess my arms were in. All the veins in them had disappeared through injecting. I was still hot all the way through my body, I was still trembling after being prayed for. Up until this point, the thought of stopping using drugs had never crossed my mind. I loved them. But something had happened, something had changed. I wanted to be rid of them.

With my sleeves rolled up and my arms stretched towards the ceiling, I looked up, and that desire to be rid of the drugs welled up in me, and I shouted at the top of my voice, 'God, you really are there! God, you are alive! God, what have I been doing with my life?'

And I looked at my arms again, at the legacy of all those years of injecting, and I shouted, 'God, all I want to do is get this s*** out of my f****** system!'

And it was the most passionate prayer I had ever prayed. I totally meant it. I did swear, but at the time I don't think God cared. He heard the cry of my heart! My experience that morning had left me hungry to be rid of all the rubbish I'd had in my system for so long.

At the time I was on 55 ml of methadone a day; I'd been taking it for years and now I wanted to get off it. The next day, Monday, I took 20 ml of methadone instead of 55, and I thought I would withdraw, but I didn't. Up until this point all my get up and go had got up and gone. That's what drugs do to you. An addict has to have his drugs to be able to cope with even simple things. Going shopping or taking the dog out for a walk had been about as much as I could do. But after that first day in church, I found that I was just brimming with energy. I felt like I was full of drive and vision and passion again.

Later that day John called to ask if I was going to hear Noel Proctor speak. I said yes. When we arrived at Dearnley Methodist Church it was completely different from the church I had been to on the Sunday. This was my idea of a church, with traditional wooden pews. I sat there with John on the third row from the front. Noel didn't recognize me; it had been years since I had last been in Strangeways, and Noel had seen thousands pass through the prison gates in his time.

He took the whole meeting and then, after singing and leading the people in a few songs, he spoke and explained about what Jesus did on the cross and why – that he had died for our sins. And as he was speaking I had a similar experience to the one I had had on the Sunday. I was hot all the way through, I was shaking, I was crying. This was nothing to do with cold turkey. I wasn't feeling ill or aching in any way. I felt great.

What's this? I thought. *It must be God again.*

I sat there for some time listening to Noel and then he said: 'If you want to receive Christ into your life, I want you to come out of your seat and come and kneel at the rail here.'

I didn't understand at the time what all this meant but I believed it, and God was truly on my case. And I wanted him more than anything in the world. I was the first to get up there! I felt like I'd been pinged out of my seat. It was like God had taken me by the scruff of the neck and got me on my feet and up to that rail; and when I got there I knelt down. A man called Roy from the church came and stood with me and led me in a prayer. He asked me to repeat it after him. So I did. As I was asking God to forgive my sin, and asking Jesus to come into my life, tears were running down my face. I was trembling. I couldn't help it.

I walked out of that meeting absolutely beaming. My face was bright red. I was on fire!

That same week after becoming a Christian I went round to John's house. Janet, the wife of Howard the worship leader, did a Christian course there one afternoon a week. That day she was teaching about the third person of the Trinity – the Holy Spirit. After she had finished speaking, she and the group prayed for me, and in an instant I was filled with the Spirit and started to speak in tongues – so I was doing what Howard and Samuel had been doing in church. I couldn't believe this. It was supernatural!

In the morning before going to church with Dot, I had taken 55 ml of methadone. The next day I cut down to 20 ml, and I felt no withdrawal symptoms. After shouting out to God, my aim was to drop it down by 5 ml a week, so that in four weeks I would be off it completely, and I

did. It was only with the last 5 ml that I felt a bit of dis-
comfort; but it wasn't that bad, certainly not like when I
was hallucinating and climbing up the walls at Platt
Lane police station years before; it wasn't full-on withdrawals by any means. I was sleeping, I was out and
about, and I didn't have any pain in my legs. It was just
uncomfortable.

After that I started to attend the Sunday and midweek
meetings of the church, which I discovered was called
the Branches Christian Fellowship. Alan Reeve, the
leader, was a former Methodist minister. The midweek
meetings were at different people's houses, and he used
to pick me up in his van and take me wherever we needed to go.

Before I attended the church for the first time, I used
to fill my days by watching TV. But now that didn't
interest me any more. I thought, *I'm going to get rid of my
TV and my video. I'm going to study and learn about God.*

All I wanted to do was learn about God. I found the
Bible fascinating, I couldn't put it down. I got a small
study desk and put it in my living-room, and I used to
study the Bible for eight hours a day. Alan gave me various notes to follow, and told me the way to read the
Bible. If I came across a bit that I didn't understand, I
used to write it down and then at the end of the day I
would ring Alan and ask him lots of questions. Alan
always had time for me. He was patient and a great pastor. Even then I think he sensed that God had a clear and
strong purpose for my life.

I was incredibly hungry for God, and when I wasn't
reading my Bible I was praying. That was how I filled
my days. I was still on benefits and not working, so I
used all my time to develop my relationship with God.

Alan then started a men's nurture group with John
and I, and we worked through the basics of the faith.

There were only the three of us in the group and I realize now that he did this just for me. I also attended the general Bible studies that the church did during the day and in the evenings. I couldn't get enough of it.

My Doctor, Samuel Yangye, was one of the leaders in the church. He did this as well as his work at the hospital. I used to go round to his house, and his wife Betty used to make us tea. He also believed that God had called me for a reason and that I had a clear call on my life. After all that I had been through, it was good that Samuel, my doctor, believed this. This wasn't another breakdown, or a drug-induced state. This was God, and he knew it!

After four weeks I came off the methadone and the prescription drugs. I wasn't using anything at all – it was the first time I had done this since I was 17. I was full of life. I decided that I was going to see Samuel, to tell him that I wasn't hearing voices any more and that I didn't need my medication. I made an appointment, thinking it would be easy, because I knew Samuel and he was aware of what had happened to me. But when I walked in, someone else was sitting there. Samuel had moved to another hospital.

I told this other doctor that I wasn't hearing the voices any more and I didn't need my Stelazine, and I told him that I had stopped taking my methadone. Now, nobody ever says these sorts of things to their doctor, so he said to me, 'Why don't you need these drugs any more?'

And I said, 'I've become a Christian and God's healed me.'

And he looked at me for a long time, looking kind of wary. He went out of the room, and then came back, and I just sat waiting for him.

Now, coming off medication also meant that I would have to come off benefits. I wasn't worried about this, because by now I was thinking that God had a plan for me, and I knew he was going to take care of everything for me. I didn't know how it was going to work out, but I believed that if I was willing to give up all my social security, then God would take care of me.

So the doctor said, 'Okay, but we will watch you. Will you come back next month?'

So I did that; I went back the following month and told him that same story. This was in 1995. The doctor declared me fit and sent me away; I've not seen a psychiatrist since then!

During this time I decided that I should give up smoking; I tried to do this straight away, but without smoking I felt really rough. Then after six weeks, one day I woke up, picked up my tobacco tin to roll a smoke, and thought, *I don't need this tobacco; I don't need it any more.* I threw it all away into the bin, and I have never smoked since. I didn't get any kind of withdrawals, I just stopped.

Some after becoming a Christian I called my mam and dad to tell them. My dad picked up the phone and I said, 'Dad, I've become a Christian.'

And I could almost feel him on the other end of the phone, wondering what this was all about. My dad knew me, he knew about all the stuff that I had been through. I could just imagine his face, his eyes rolling as I told him, and him thinking, *Whatever, whatever.*

Shortly after this I went to see them. They were watching the telly and I sat on the floor. I was buzzing with enthusiasm. My life was on fire. I looked up to my dad, who was reading his paper.

I said, 'Dad, do you realize what God could do with someone like me? You know, one day I am going to write a book.'

I think at this stage he wasn't prepared to believe that this was a serious transformation of my life. But I have written a book, and this is it.

And it's a story worth telling because I know the difference between the deception of drugs and the reality of God freeing me. I know what cold turkey is; I know what it's like to be off my face; I know when I'm sick and when I'm well. And I was sick, and now I am well. I know that what's happened to me is real and true, and only God could have done it.

If I'd tried to come off my prescription drugs like this without God, it would have crippled me; I wouldn't have been able to get out of bed. But in fact I had, and still have, more energy than ever before. I was sick and now I am well; I had been an addict, but now I was drug free.

Chapter 14

Clear Calling

The morning I walked into that church, life changed for me. I'd had an encounter with God. The way that I talked changed; the bad language that I had used ever since I could remember just stopped. Even some of the street slang that I had used for years disappeared. I also started to talk more positively about things in general. The way that I thought changed; I didn't think about drugs any more. I was thinking more about normal things, and about my purpose in life. The way that I acted changed. Some of my familiar mannerisms stopped and even my manners were different. I wasn't the same person that I was. My life was now consumed with God. All the passion that I used to have for drugs was now being channelled towards God. He became my everything.

During the time that I spent reading the Bible and praying, I had an overwhelming sense that God was calling me. It was too obvious to miss. I started to think of the experience that I had had in Buxton three years before, when I thought that God had called me. That had been the awakening of something in me, some kind of calling from God. In the state I was in at the time, a lot of what I thought and felt was just me, not God. Now it was different; now I had a clearer understanding of what it was to be passionate for God.

I'd been a Christian for about two months when someone from church gave me a tape to listen to. It was the story of a woman who used to be a witch, but now she's a Christian. Her name is Doreen Irvine, and her story is called *From Witchcraft to Christ*. One afternoon, after I had spent the morning reading my Bible, I decided to listen to this tape. I put it into the player and listened with great interest. I was gripped by this powerful story, and then Doreen said that God had called her to be an evangelist. As she said this, the words hit me like a ton of bricks.

That's it, I thought. *That's what God has called me to do!*

And this time I meant it. Christians will often talk about a really deep conviction concerning what God wants them to do – that is their calling. I knew without any doubt, that this was my calling; this was what God wanted me to do.

After finishing the tape I called Alan. By this time I had already had some discussions with him about what I could do with my life. I remember him saying to me one day, 'It's not what you want to do, it's what God wants you to do.' He never tried to put any ideas in my mind; he was waiting until I heard God for myself.

He picked up the phone and I didn't say 'Hello' or 'How are you?' or anything. I just burst out with, 'Alan, I know what it is that God has called me to do!'

There was a slight pause and so I continued, 'God's called me to be an evangelist!'

There was another pause. 'Huh, okay.' That's all he said; nothing more.

'Alan,' I said.

'Yes?'

'What's an evangelist?'

I knew I was called, but I didn't know what an evangelist was. I didn't have a clue. Alan didn't get excited and he didn't even tell me what an evangelist was. He just said calmly, 'Okay, we can pray that through,' and then put the phone down.

I couldn't understand why he had responded like he did, but this was it. God had called me to be an evangelist. I knew without a doubt that this was my purpose.

I asked questions and read a few books as well as the Bible, and I pretty soon worked out what the role of an evangelist was. An evangelist is a person who proclaims the Christian faith with simplicity and clarity so that individuals can understand it and respond by believing and accepting Jesus Christ as their number one. In other words, by making him Lord of their life. Evangelists are communicators of the Christian message, and some even pray for sick people and God heals through them. I soon learned that God had often called people with a similar background to mine to do this type of work.

Then, for a while, it seemed as if I was hearing about evangelists all the time. For a period of about six weeks, after I had first heard God speak to me through the Doreen Irvine tape, I kept hearing about this particular calling. I'd put a tape on, and it was an evangelist speaking. I'd open a book, and the word 'evangelist' was there on the page. I remember being in a house that had the TV on, and in the programme they were talking about an evangelist. I went to see my parents once, and my dad gave me a video that he had taped the night before because he thought I might be interested. I asked him what it was; he said it was about Billy Graham. My dad isn't even a Christian!

I was invited to go and hear an evangelist speak in a church in Rochdale. I hadn't seen one live before. He was called Stephen George and he came from India. He only came to the UK once a year. After he had finished speaking he started to pray for people who were ill. I watched with great interest. As well as speaking to everyone together, he also walked up to some individuals and spoke specific words to them from God. I had never seen anything like it before. I was sat at the back of the church, and he looked over at me, and then came walking my way. He was very gentle and quietly spoken. He looked me in the eyes with a smile on his face and said, 'God is going to use you to deliver many others as you yourself have been delivered.'

Then he walked away. I was amazed. Here was this guy, all the way from India; he didn't know me from Adam, and he said this! *How does he know that I have been delivered from drugs? How does he know that God has called me to be an evangelist?* These were the thoughts that were going through my mind. I realized that this was yet another confirmation. I knew for sure that these weren't just coincidences but 'Godincidences'. I was becoming more and more certain of my calling. It was so clear.

At the same time, while all this was going on, other strange things were happening. There was one incident when I was lying on my bed in the afternoon and I had my eyes closed. I was still awake; and as I lay there, the room filled with the brightest light you have ever seen. And then I 'saw' two angels standing around the bed; they were as white as snow, and they looked so over-joyed and excited. They were moving around the bed, while I was lying there. I later read in the Bible about how angels celebrate over one person who finds God.

As I continued my intense study, I also felt that God was calling me to Bible college. I was so hungry for the things of God that I wanted all that I could get. I mentioned this to Alan, and he agreed that this would be good for me and that it was of God. I had messed up with education first time around when I was at school, but now I had a second chance. I sent off for some prospectuses for different Bible colleges, and the one where I truly felt I needed to be was Cliff College in Derbyshire, and that was because they offered training for evangelists. This was a Methodist College, but they accepted students from any church background, which was helpful for me, coming from an independent church. Again I chatted this through with Alan and talked to Howard and Samuel, the other leaders in the church, and they all agreed that this was the way forward.

I began praying, and the church was praying as well, and there was general agreement that this was indeed what God was saying to me. I put in my application and shortly after that I got a letter from Cliff College asking me to come for an interview.

At this time I was still on benefits, but I knew that at some point I would be coming off them. I also knew that if I was going to Bible college I would have to give up my flat, give my furniture away, and find a good home for my dog. I was ready to do whatever it took, because I knew the real adventure was just beginning.

It was also around this time that I asked Alan to baptize me. 'I think it best that we wait,' he said. 'This will give you time to grow and fully understand what you are doing.'

So in 1996 I was baptized in Hollingworth Lake in Rochdale. We had a brilliant day. The weather was nice and there were lots of people around to see it. This was the first time I had ever spoken in a public setting. Alan asked me to tell some of my story. When I opened my mouth, I felt so passionate and warm as I spoke; I wasn't shy and enjoyed every minute of it. Also my mam was there. After all the stuff I had put her through, she was now there to witness her son getting baptized!

Soon after my baptism, Alan picked me up at the flat to take me for my interview at Cliff College. We drove along, chatting for a while, and then I started to look out of the window at the roads and surroundings that were passing us by. I suddenly realized that I had been down these roads before. Then I saw the signs for Buxton. These were the same roads that I had driven down in 1992 when I felt that God was leading me there! My experience at the Pavilion Gardens came back to me: walking through the water, feeling clean, falling back into the water and coming out the other side, different, excited – new life! This had to be God, except this time I would get it right, and really know his will for me. Eventually we turned off and headed towards Calver, which isn't far from Buxton; but I'd recognized and received yet another confirmation that I was on track.

When we got to the college I was overwhelmed by the place. The grounds were well kept and it had a top-class feel to it. It was in a beautiful location. We walked through the grounds past one of the classrooms and I looked through the window and thought, *This is it. This is where God wants me to be.*

Then I thought back to the time when I had looked through the window at the Pavilion Gardens, and had seen the recording equipment. At the time I thought about the Pavilion Gardens as the place where God wanted me to be; then I remembered knocking on the door and saying, 'God has brought me here. God has called me.'

That was all well and good, but this was it, this was the real deal. Even the buildings looked like they did on that night when I was caught naked in Buxton. We walked through the entrance and up to the principal's office. His name was Howard Mellor.

In the interview he asked me about my former education, my conversion, and what I believed God was calling me to do. I told him what I was telling everyone else: that God had called me to be an evangelist. He then asked Alan about this and Alan supported me totally. He asked me about how I was going to finance my time at Cliff. I told him that God would provide for me. I had no doubt about that.

At the end of the interview Howard said he would give me a place, but not this year. At first I was really disappointed, but I figured that if I had to wait twelve months to get a place, then I would, because this was where God wanted me to be.

After I had been told that I had to wait a year, Alan and I started to look at other options. We sent off for more information about various courses, but none of them seemed right. Then one day Alan came round to the flat with some information about an organization called the Northern Evangelical Trust (NET). I looked at the brochure and discovered that NET was an organization that did evangelism in the North of England. They did practical training and some theological training too. They worked in schools, they did local church missions, tent missions, summer camps, everything. I thought it looked really good, really practical – just what I needed. So I applied and got an interview.

Again, Alan drove me there, and we pulled up in an old mill town near Blackburn in Lancashire. Alan parked the van outside some millstone houses and then we headed into a Christian bookshop that was on the main road. The organization was based above this shop.

The director was a guy called Brian Jackson. Brian was in his forties, with straight black hair with flecks of grey. He had a broad Lancashire accent and a tattoo on his hand. He was wearing trainers, tracksuit bottoms and a T-shirt with a collar. His office was basic and quite untidy. It was very different from the collegiate atmosphere at Cliff.

Brian was as down to earth as they come. A real character, he was full of energy and ideas about how to develop the ministry. He was a very positive, optimistic guy. He often called people 'lad'. He asked me some questions and then asked why I wanted to join.

'I'm called to be an evangelist,' I told him.

'Well, you're in the right place, lad,' he said. 'That's what we do here. Everything we do is about evangelism.' When he spoke he was really enthusiastic about it. You could tell he loved what he was doing.

He told me that NET would cover the accommodation cost and provide the food; all they asked was that my church would give me a small allowance each month. This was much less than I had been getting from my benefits.

Brian took us back round the corner to where the car was parked and showed us into a big stone house which was on the corner. 'Townley House', it was called. This was where the team lived. It hadn't been decorated for years, it was basic and untidy, and the team members shared the rooms. I remember walking out and going back to Alan's van and thinking, *This is nothing like the college, but this is where I need to be. I can learn so much from these guys.*

Alan and I chatted about it on the way home, and he agreed that this place would be good for me. So I gave Brian a call and told him I wanted to start. My plan was to spend one year there and then go to Cliff College after that. I still had my dog and the flat, and I was due to start in September of that year, 1996.

Over the next weeks I came off my benefits, I found a new home for my dog, I gave up my flat, donated all my furniture to charity and then moved into Townley House. One thing I did know was that I wasn't going back. This was just the beginning of something great for me.

As well as Brian, the NET team was run by a guy called David Shore. Dave was in his mid thirties, was about five feet nine tall and had a gap between his two front teeth. Before becoming a Christian, he had been a bit of an alcoholic and a fighter. He was a real character. He was the main evangelist on the team.

After we had been there a few days, Brian took all of us first years to a tent mission that NET had organized in Todmorden. I couldn't wait. When we arrived there was a big 500-seat marquee up on the playing field; there was a worship group and I could feel a real buzz about the place. The tent was packed.

After the music someone told their story and then Dave got up to speak. Apart from Stephen George, the Indian guy, I had never seen another evangelist in action. Dave blew me away. This was a different style altogether from Stephen's. He used lots of humour, telling jokes, doing Clint Eastwood impressions. He used a lot of his own story in what he said, but the message of Christianity was right at the centre.

After he had spoken he asked everybody to stand, and after he had prayed a short prayer, he told everyone that if they wanted to receive Christ into their life, then they should come and stand at the front. There was no music playing, just complete silence, and then after about two minutes there was the sound of the grass moving underneath people's feet as they made their way to the front. There were maybe thirty of them. To see so many respond was great.

I had tears in my eyes and a lump in my throat as they walked forward. Watching people take that first step was the best thing I had ever seen. And I was also thinking, *WOW! This is what God has called me to do. This is what I'm going to be doing.*

During one of the training sessions in our induction week Brian asked us, 'Is there anybody here who thinks they are called to be an evangelist?'

'I am,' I answered, straight away; I was the first and only person to respond.

After our initial training each of the new arrivals was placed in one of the various teams. Some were sent to spend their year serving just one church somewhere in the North of England, but I was put on the service team. Our focus was to travel to various places and do tent missions, camps and schools mission. We even worked at events like Spring Harvest. This really did open my eyes to good public speaking. I was so glad they put me on this team – it suited me.

Dave Shore had done some training on message preparation. He taught us the basics of communication and he gave us all some homework to do: how to break a Bible passage down and then how to deliver it. I loved it. I would go back to my room and spend all my free time working on it.

The service teams manager was a guy called Kevin Mott. Kevin was another straight-talking, genuine guy.

One time the team were leading a service in a Baptist church in Blackburn and I was given the chance to speak. Apart from the time I shared some of my story at my baptism, this was my first ever attempt at public speaking.

The rest of the guys organized a drama and a few other bits to contribute to the service, and I was given ten to fifteen minutes to talk. I remember that as I began to speak, I got so passionate – it was like something came over me, like a hot blanket. I seemed to change when I was speaking. I could see Kevin's face; he looked pleasantly shocked. I spoke for fifteen minutes and then I asked people if they wanted to receive Christ into their life. At that point people came to the front. People were in tears, crying and shaking; it was like there was a huge cloud of smoke on the platform. There were all kinds of people in there: doctors, solicitors, you name it – they were there! God's presence came into the building in such a strong way. You could feel it. It was a powerful time.

When we were driving home Kevin was so excited. He said there was no doubt about it that I was an evangelist. 'God has anointed you, mate! I can't wait to tell Brian and Dave,' he said.

The next morning Brian came into the offices, and Kevin had already told him. He had phoned him after the meeting. He was really excited.

'I heard it went well, last night,' he said.

'Yes,' I said, 'it was amazing.'

Over that year David Shore took me under his wing and helped me to learn some more about speaking publicly to non-Christians. I think he enjoyed having someone like me to train and spend time with. As the year went on, I was given many opportunities to speak at various events, and when the tent-mission season started around April, Brian and Dave let me speak at these too. They recognized God's call on my life and they didn't want to get in the way. Every time I spoke, people would respond. Kevin Mott would sometimes sacrifice his own chances to speak in order to give me more opportunities, so I could gain more experience.

I had such a good time that I didn't want to leave. I did every kind of evangelism under the sun; they had taught me loads. They had invested in me and I had got on well with them. But I knew that this was only for a short season, because my sights were set on going to Cliff. And so in September 1997 I said goodbye to the NET team.

Chapter 15

Trained and Equipped

During the six weeks between leaving the NET team and starting at Bible college, I lived in a community house in Rochdale. The house was owned by two friends of mine, Alan and Margaret Mew. They knew that I had given up my flat and they had said I could stay with them, free of charge. Their community house became my home during holidays.

On 1 September 1997 I started as a student at Cliff Bible College. I had heard so much good stuff about the place that I couldn't wait to start. At my interview the principal had said I could have a place for a one-year certificate course, but I dreamed of doing more than a year there. I thought that I might be able to do a second year, which would give me a diploma in evangelism, but at this stage the thought of doing a degree was out of the question.

A friend from church called Wayne gave me an old Mark 1 Ford Escort. It wasn't the best of cars, but at least it got me back on the road again and provided me with transport while I was a student. When I arrived I was shown to my room; it was on the second floor and my window overlooked the college lawn. As I looked out on that first day, the sun was shining, the birds were singing, and I just thought of God's grace to me. I had never lived anywhere like this; it was a beautiful place.

At first I was a bit overwhelmed by college life. I thought of where I had come from and the kind of life I had lived; and now here I was, a student at Bible college, right in the heart of the Peak District.

There were about sixty other first-year students who started on the same day as I did, and most of them had completely different backgrounds from me. Some of my peers had just finished 'A' Levels and yet here I was, in the same class, and I didn't even have Maths and English GCSE!

What I did have was a conviction that this was the place where God wanted me to be, and I was absolutely determined that I was going to make the best of it. I had messed up my education first time around, and now I had a second chance and I was not going to waste it.

During the first few days at the college the new arrivals were taken through an induction process. As a part of this we were taken to the Computer Room. One of the tutors, Paul Ashby, was with us that day and he asked if there was anybody who wasn't familiar with IT. I looked around and there was one older guy called Victor, who was in his sixties, who put his hand up. I thought, *IT? What does that mean?* I didn't have a clue, so I put my hand up as well. I had spent some time programming drum machines and synthesizers in the past, but I had no experience at all with computers. It was just another challenge that I would have to face.

Each student was assigned to a house group, and my group was run by Andy Smith. Andy was an evangelist employed by the college to work on that aspect of the training. The group met at Andy's house which was on the college grounds. The first time I went there, I walked into his living-room and immediately noticed that in a corner of the room was a pair of Technics turntables. It turned out that Andy was into dance music. I told him that I was once into it too, but that was all in the past.

At my first house-group meeting, Andy gave each of us a piece of A5 paper and asked us to write a letter, addressed to ourselves, using one side of the paper. In this letter we were to write about our hopes and fears for the coming year. We each wrote our letter, put it in an envelope and gave it to him. I soon forgot about the letter and focused instead on my studies.

Sometimes, after the house-group meetings had finished, I would have a play on Andy's Technics decks and I discovered that I could still mix.

When the lectures started I really enjoyed them; I had a great appetite for the teaching. I was the most enthusiastic student in the class; I'd be first in and I'd sit in the front row, ready for them to start.

Our first assignment was to write out our testimony. I could not use the computer, so I wrote it all out by hand. My grammar wasn't very good and I had to use a ruler to keep my writing straight. Despite this, I got quite a decent mark. I got a good mark for my second assignment as well, and I began to realize that I really could do this sort of academic work.

My next assignment stretched me a bit more. I had to write a longer essay, that required even more research. I quickly learnt how to find references and identify sources of information; and I discovered that I really enjoyed this sort of work. Doing these assignments convinced me that I had to learn to use the computer. I had written a couple of essays by hand, but then I discovered that Richard, who was in the room next to mine, was really good at typing. I did all the work by hand and then asked him if he would type it out for me if I gave him £10. The tutors were happy with this arrangement, provided I did all the work.

I was thinking about my need to learn to use the computer when, out of the blue, I got a cheque through the post for £150. I bought a basic second-hand computer with Microsoft Word software and got to work. It took me some time to learn how to use it, but with Richard's help I was soon able to use the basic functions. I was able to type my third assignment myself.

After finishing my first few assignments, I realized that I was actually well suited to the academic demands placed on me by the college. I was getting very good marks: fourteen or fifteen out of sixteen.

Each student had a personal tutor and mine was Howard Mellor, the principal. One day we were discussing my progress at the college. 'I hear things are going well for you, Barry,' he said.

'Yes they are, Howard,' I said. 'I'm enjoying the course and I seem to be getting good marks.'

'You are,' said Howard. 'In fact, we would like to offer you a place on the three-year degree course, rather than just the basic one-year certificate course.'

I was really chuffed to get this offer and I told him that I would let him know. It didn't take me long to make up my mind, and the next day I said yes, and transferred to the degree course.

I continued to work hard, obtaining good marks. On top of all my core modules, I opted to do a research project on preaching, as well as a homiletics course. Homiletics is the study of speaking and preaching, and at the time the course was run by Martyn Atkins, who became the next principal of the college. I also retook my English GCSE and passed.

During the first year I was able to get some further practical experience in mission. My first mission was at

Easter, and Andy Smith, my house-group leader, led the team. He gave me full marks for my efforts on the mission and said in his comments that 'Barry Woodward is a born evangelist.'

All in all, I had a great first year, and I was proud to receive my certificate at the graduation ceremony. Even those on the three-year degree course get presented with a Cliff College certificate at the end of their first year. After the ceremony I went back to my room to pick up my bags and load them into the car. When I went into my room I saw an envelope on the floor; it had obviously been pushed under the door by someone.

It was the letter I had written to myself at the beginning of the year; I had forgotten all about it. I picked up the envelope, sat on the bed and opened it. This is what it said:

Dear Barry

I am writing this letter to tell you what my fears and expectations are at Cliff.

I hope during my 1st year that my English will improve both in speech and in written work. I hope to become more holy and grow in my knowledge of God. I pray that I will do well on this course and be accepted onto Level Two. I need confidence in my academic work and I ask God for that. I pray that my knowledge of evangelism will grow. I pray that I will receive more anointing.

I have so many fears and hopes for the year; they could fill much more than this small piece of paper.

Reading it again, and remembering how nervous I had been at the start of the year, I could see that God had fulfilled all of my aspirations. I had acquired my English GCSE and I had grown in my knowledge of God. I had learned so much about evangelism and I had been accepted onto the second year (and even the third!). I was able to thank God that all my hopes had been fulfilled.

At the start of the year I had felt overwhelmed by my own lack of ability and intimidated by the people around me – they all seemed much more capable than me. I should have had more confidence in God, even if I did not have confidence in myself, because at the end of what was a very good year for me, I had an excellent overall mark and I was awarded a prize for being the best New Testament Student. I looked forward to the next academic year with more confidence and expectation about what God would do.

The second year at Cliff was very different from the first. The course was more practical, with a focus on leadership training and missions. Second-year students usually lead the first-years on missions. Also during the second year, students had to prepare a 12,000-word dissertation. I did mine on 'Effective Evangelistic Preaching Today'. I had the whole year to think about this subject and write it up; as a part of my research I interviewed some of the UK's best evangelistic communicators. For me this was a time to learn as much as I could about communicating the Christian faith in a relevant and effective way. I was highly motivated because I knew that this was what I was going to spend the rest of my life doing.

I continued with my second year as I had started with the first, really enjoying the course, and I came home to the community house at the end of the first term for Christmas, feeling very positive. During the holiday God began to give me a clearer picture of what he had in mind for me. I was reading a book in my room one day, and the author used an illustration to describe the idea of hitting a window of opportunity.

In the illustration, he described how Richard Branson was hoping to go round the world in a hot-air balloon using a particular wind-current. If the balloon hit that current at the right time and in the right place, it would be able to fly round the world.

At around this time, I was wondering about whether I needed to be at Cliff for three years. All my fees for the first year had been paid; and I had funds available to pay for the second year. God had provided them, as I believed he would when I went for the interview. It was at this time that everybody was talking about evangelistic opportunities in the year 2000. I loved being at college, but I was only there to get the tools in my tool-box so I could be effective as an evangelist. I didn't want to get caught up with academia, I just wanted to get out there and get on with the job.

As I was reading this book a question came to my mind: *Do I need to be at Bible college for three years, or should I graduate after two and leave with a diploma instead of a degree?*

I was already busy with a number of speaking engagements during the holiday periods between college terms. There were invitations arriving for me to get involved in missions, especially with the year 2000 coming up.

The morning after reading about the balloon, I was watching the news in the TV room, and the first thing that came on was a piece about Richard Branson flying his hot-air balloon around the world for a second time! The feature described the challenge that Branson faced. If he could set off on his journey from the right place and at the right moment – if he could hit that window of opportunity – he would catch the wind and it would carry him all the way round the world. Watching this news item, I thought, *That's it! That's the confirmation. I need to hit this window of opportunity. The year 2000 is going to be crucial, and I don't want to miss God's window.*

I really believed that I needed to leave college, not with a BA degree but with a diploma. The course at Cliff was structured to allow students who had completed two years to receive a diploma. This meant that I would receive a qualification at the end of my two years, even if I wasn't going to stay and finish the degree.

When I went back to college after Christmas, the first thing I did was to make an appointment to see the principal, Howard Mellor. I said to Howard, 'Listen, I'm going to leave at the end of this academic year.'

Howard looked at me over his glasses and said, 'Hmm. Why is that, then?'

I told him how God had been speaking to me, and I told him about the hot-air balloon story and that I believed that God wanted me to hit the window of opportunity presented by the millennium. Howard asked a few more questions and then he said, 'Okay. I believe that's God.'

Now, a college principal would not normally say that; usually, if you are that far into the course, they like you to finish; but to his credit, Howard believed that this was right, and he never questioned it.

Throughout my time at college I was asking God how he wanted me to work when I left. I knew that I was going to be a full-time evangelist, but I wasn't sure about how this was going to be funded or whether it was going to be with an organization or whatever. I was busy weighing up the options.

I looked at how other evangelists operated and I really felt that God was leading me to set up my own charity. I met up with some of them to get their advice and to look at the best way forward; then, while I was still a student, I decided to set up my own trust. This way, I would be accountable to trustees and all the finance for ministry would be put in the trust. It would also give me the freedom to work with different denominations and networks.

I did all the research and wrote to the Charity Commission and then I went about preparing a trust deed. I approached three trustees and I asked a number of people to be on my council of reference; and then I asked Janet Smith, the wife of my church's worship leader, Howard Smith, to be our first administrator. She agreed. Janet did a lot of work to help me get the whole project off the ground.

The timing was perfect. Four weeks before I was due to graduate, everything was complete and in place for the trust to function. I came to the end of my second year in the summer of 1999 and, on my graduation day, I became the Director of Proclaim Trust. I had developed a mission statement to express as clearly as possible the aim of the Trust. It reads:

> The purpose of Proclaim Trust is to serve the local church in the area of evangelism, by communicating the good news and preparing God's people for mission.

This second graduation day was a great experience for me. I had invited my trustees and some of my board members. I had also invited my mam and dad. After all that I had put them through, it was so good for them to see me graduating from Bible college. At last I had given them a reason to be proud of me. I collected my diploma, and looked forward to getting on with what God had called me to do: to be an evangelist.

Chapter 16

On a Mission

The day I left college, I started work with the Trust. We had £10 in the bank. I moved back to Rochdale to live with Alan and Margaret. They gave me a big room, and that became my office and my bedroom, and I ran the Trust from there.

While I was at college I'd received quite a lot of invitations to speak, both in the UK and overseas at various types of missions and events. One of the things that I was keen to do was to work with different denominations and networks; I believed that this was important for an evangelist. Billy Graham once said that he 'preaches the cross and not a denomination'; and even though there is a more charismatic edge to my ministry, I wanted to follow his example.

Four days after leaving Bible college, I travelled to Germany to be the main speaker at a two-week mission with the Vineyard Church in Nuremberg; they also invited a band over from the States to do the music. The church hired a large room at the back of a café in the centre of town. Each night the meetings were packed. Throughout the two weeks we saw many people take their first step towards God, and many were healed and filled with the Holy Spirit.

While I was in Germany, I was introduced to a Christian organization called the 'Jesus Freaks'. This movement had been born out of the punk-rock scene, and the way they did church was totally different from anything else I had experienced. I'd never seen punk-rock music used in worship before, and I was glad to get the opportunity to speak to this group.

Early on in my ministry I felt God begin to challenge me about going back to my own 'personal Egypt' – that is, the people that I was a part of – to reach them. There is a guy in the Bible called Moses. He was a Hebrew, but he was brought up in Egypt and so he understood the language and the culture of that particular group. One day, after he had moved out of Egypt, God sent him back to release the Hebrew people. I felt that God was asking me to do the same thing, but my own personal Egypt was the club scene.

While I was at Cliff College I had started doing a bit of DJ-ing again. I had discovered that I could use this as a tool to communicate the Christian faith, so I began to collect twelve-inch records again, together with some other bits of vinyl that I could sample live while doing a set. My favourite was an old LP that I had found that was full of Martin Luther King's talks. I played all the latest dance music stuff, and this gave me credibility with the people I was trying to reach.

I pursued this because I knew that I could reach a particular people group. I had totally lost interest in music by this time, but I knew that I had this skill and that it could be used for God, and I believed that this was something that he wanted me to do, even if this was only going to be for a short season. My main activity was still going to be public speaking.

One night I was flicking through some channels on the TV, and I saw a programme called *Ibiza Uncovered*. I watched it for about ten minutes and what I saw troubled me; this really was extreme hedonism. The content of the programme stayed with me over the next few days, and then finally I thought, *Ibiza is where I need to go.*

This was the place where I could go and reach many of the kind of people that I used to mix with – lots of them in one go. And I could do it in the year 2000. These were my kind of people and this was my window of opportunity!

There were a number of things that confirmed this as God's plan. At this time, nobody had been into Ibiza to do this type of mission; but I would not go there unless I could work with local churches or Christian organizations; I would never go it alone. I made some enquiries and established a connection with the English-speaking Anglican church on Ibiza. They were really keen and asked me to come over and meet them and have a chat. They said that they were praying for the island and that they had been asking God to send them help.

I flew over and spent some time with a guy called Art. At that time he was acting as the leader in the church while they were waiting for their new minister to arrive. Art was from New Zealand and he and his wife ran a family restaurant. I stayed for a week in January 2000, and during that time I drove round the island having a look around, and thinking up a strategy for outreach. While I was there I spoke at various meetings and I ran an evangelism-training day with the people from the church, so that they could join in with the mission.

After I arrived back in the UK, I went about making plans for me to return with a team in the summer of that year. For our first trip to Ibiza, I gathered ten team members, all from different backgrounds.

We had a guy with us called Barry Johnson. Some weeks before I went out to Ibiza, I had done a mission in

Bradford, and I had spoken at an outreach event, where I was introduced to him. Before he became a Christian Barry had been an alcoholic and a drug dealer. At five feet eight he wasn't very tall, but he was a strong bloke and he was stocky and broad. He had short hair, and tattoos all over his body. He used to be a boxer and he had a flat nose. In his time he had been a bouncer, and he was also into break-dancing – and that's what I needed him for in Ibiza.

Then there was David Blair. In 1999 I had been invited to be the speaker at a week-long mission at Lancaster University. This was where I met Dave. He had an interesting past too. In the eighties he had been part of a gang in Manchester called the Quality Street Gang. In their heyday these guys were pure gangsters. Later David had become a Christian; he was a very strong character and he was also a big guy, about six foot six.

We also had some girls on the team. There was Amy, who had come from a church background. She was 21 years old and she was really enthusiastic about her Christian faith. She loved God and she loved people – a really nice girl. Then there was another girl called Lou. Lou was calm and gentle; she was also about 21 at the time. She was totally committed to her faith and to our mission.

One thing I found when I started to draw teams together for work in Ibiza was that there were a lot of people who said they were 'called' to work there. I would get phone calls out of the blue, and it would be someone who had heard that I was taking a team to work with clubbers in the dance-music capital of the world. Then they would ask if they could join the team, because they felt called.

My reply would often be: 'Well, I'm doing a week's mission on a council estate in Manchester next month; did you want to be part of that team?'

Their reply would often be: 'No, I'm not called to do that.'

So I'd simply say: 'If you're not willing to do that, then maybe Ibiza isn't for you either.'

I didn't want people to come just because it sounded glamorous – although there was an element of glamour to it. The reality was that the mission would be hard work. The criterion for each team member was that they had to be on fire for God. I didn't mind anything else. I knew that these people would not be swayed by the heady Ibiza atmosphere.

Before we went, we had two preparation weekends together. The purpose of this was threefold. First, I wanted to give people some training on how to share the gospel in a non-directive, non-aggressive way; secondly, I wanted us to bond as a team; and finally, I wanted to give everyone time to rehearse our programme – when we did our stuff out there, it had to be good.

We arrived on the island and put our plans into action.

While I was on the pre-mission trip, I had been introduced to the chief of police of San Antonio. He happened to be a Christian who attended the Spanish-speaking evangelical church on the island. He put in a good word for us, so we were able to get permission to run our programme from 9 p.m. to 12 midnight every night on the streets of San Antonio.

I would DJ live on the streets, and mix in Christian samples of people speaking over the music, while the crowd stood around listening. We had two girls on the team who were vocalists and they would sing live over the music. Again, what they were singing reflected what we believed. We also had an artist on the team. She would be working on an abstract piece of art while all this was going on, and Barry was doing his break-dancing. This really did draw the crowds. While the people were standing around, the rest of the team members were chatting to people about Christianity. Some of the punters couldn't believe that we were Christians. We'd had some trendy business cards made with a contact email address, and we gave these out to anyone who wanted to chat some more at a later date. Every night we would draw a crowd. Some nights there were literally hundreds of people there.

At 12 midnight we would load the car up and then head off to work in the clubs. We had been introduced to some of the bar and club owners. We told them that they could have a free DJ in return for free soft drinks for the team, and most of them agreed. While I was doing my set, the team were mixing and mingling with the people, getting into conversations about God and Christianity.

We also visited 'Privilege', the largest nightclub in the world. Each night different club promoters would host events there. The biggest night on the island was held in 'Privilege' by the promoters from 'Manumission'. The management at 'Manumission' went out of their way to make their events *different*; they would do the most extreme things, and some of them I wouldn't even tell you about. We would be outside the venue from about four in the morning, just to chat to clubbers; also we would put specially designed club-style flyers on car windscreens, explaining the Christian faith.

On the Sunday, at two in the afternoon, we took all the equipment to the beach, including our generator, and set it up. Again we did our programme and let people know that this was our church. It blew people away.

When we first went to Ibiza we didn't know how people were going to respond. We were the first group to do anything like this. That's why it was good to have members like Barry and Dave on the team, just in case there was any trouble. But when we arrived and started to do our stuff, we realized that it wasn't going to be a big deal. In Ibiza you can be whatever you want to be; there are transvestites, gays, drug users, dealers – you name it, they're there! So for us to be Christians was not that radical. We were just another group being what we wanted to be.

Our first visit to Ibiza was a great success. The Anglican church there gave us some money and found us some transport and accommodation, while each member of the team made a commitment to find their own airfare and make a financial contribution to the food.

After we returned we began to make plans for two more visits in 2001. In fact, 2001 was the year when another organization, which focused mainly on prayer, sent out their first team. They had been praying about this for some time and they had also been in contact with the Anglican church on the island.

During our two missions in 2001 I had the sense that these were going to be my last trips. Now there were other organizations coming in who were willing to stay for the whole summer season. We had been given the opportunity to do this, but I couldn't give such a big commitment to the project. I had lots of other opportunities coming up and I felt that I needed to focus on them.

Back in the UK, I was given the opportunity to move the Trust into its own office. I made contact with a businessman and church leader in Rochdale called Dave. He and his wife Joyce had recently bought the big, old Methodist Central Hall in the town, and he knew about the work that I was doing, so he gave me an office free of charge. Soon after this I moved out of the community house and Dave let me rent a small flat that was on his own property.

The work in Ibiza was just one of a number of projects I had on the go. I was also travelling around the UK and overseas, doing missions where I was doing lots of public speaking. In 1999 I was invited to attend a Billy Graham conference in Amsterdam the following year called 'Amsterdam 2000'. The invite just came through the post one day. I don't know how they knew about me, but I decided to go. This gathering was amazing; there were about 12,000 of us in all, and some brilliant speakers. During this time I was able to meet up with other evangelists from different parts of the world.

Within weeks of the conference, I received an invitation to speak in Argentina. I had read so much about this place and about how they had experienced two great moves of God, so I took up the offer without hesitation. I joined a team of twenty others who were there for a two-week-long mission. The people there were hungry for God; they were so open. We saw God move in wonderful ways and many made commitments to Christ. People were filled with the Spirit and there were many supernatural healings – it was amazing.

I remember one day on this trip when I spoke seven times. I'd been taking seminars on evangelism during the day, and then in the evening I spoke at an outreach meeting that finished at about 11 p.m.

After I had finished the pastor of the church came up to me and said, 'Tonight we have an all-night evangelistic concert; will you come and preach for us? We want you to be our speaker – we like your style.'

Well, I must say I was flattered. That's a big compliment coming from an Argentine. I said that I certainly would come and speak; it would be a privilege.

I went back to the hotel, got showered and changed, and then we travelled out for about an hour to the venue. Maybe 500 people where there. There were three bands on at this concert and then I was going to be the speaker. The atmosphere was electric. I spoke, and as I gave the altar call, about 150 people came forward, and people were slain in the Spirit. There was an incredible atmosphere there that night; we could feel the presence of God like a tangible thing; it was very powerful.

After my first trip to Argentina I accepted two other invitations to go back and speak. On the second visit I was interviewed for a TV programme. I preached live over the air several times, and I was also able to get into a prison. I spoke to about 110 cons and maybe 35 of them made first-time commitments. I prayed for people and God really did move – many of the prisoners fell to the floor and prayed in the Spirit for the first time.

These missions seemed so fruitful that I began to think about going out to Argentina for six months and really focusing on what I could do there; I got on well with some of the key leaders there who were willing to make plans for me to hold various evangelistic events throughout the country. I was even thinking of learning Spanish during the six months I was there.

In 2001 I also went to Sri Lanka for six weeks, working with Hindus on the various tea plantations in what they call the 'up country'. Doug Clarke, one of my trustees, came with me on this trip. We trained leaders and spoke in churches, but my main focus was holding evangelistic meetings in the remote villages. We had a very fruitful time. Again, we saw many people take a first step towards God, and he confirmed his word with supernatural signs and wonders; these are events that cannot be explained by normal physical laws, like people being miraculously healed.

I also received an invitation to go to India. One of my board members, Revd Ernest Anderson, asked me to travel with him to take all the evangelistic meetings. I did, and again we saw God move in marvellous ways. I returned the next year with my own team.

In the years after leaving college, I was involved in quite a number of overseas missions, and when I wasn't abroad I was busy speaking around the UK at various events. Wherever I went, people would respond to the gospel message and, again depending on the type of event or setting, God would confirm his word with signs and wonders. Right from the beginning, this had been a characteristic of meetings where I spoke.

Now, even though I was busy abroad, there was always something in me that wanted to be doing more in the UK. I love my own country and I believed that because of my background, this was where God was going to use me the most. There is an element of glamour that comes from travelling to other countries. I'm not saying in any way that it's wrong to do this, and I still do travel; but at the back of mind I was always conscious of my own country. So I made a decision that I would change the focus and build up the work in Britain.

At the same time I believed that God was saying something very important to me about focusing on the heart of my mission. His words to me were: '*You need to major on your majors and minor on your minors.*'

I was going to various parts of the world doing missions. I was planning and organizing the trips to Ibiza; I was also doing a bit of DJ-ing at various events in the UK. I was visiting hostels and prisons, and doing various other types of ministry. All of this was good; but now I felt that it was time to put some of these things down and make room for the main thing that I was called to do – evangelistic preaching and, for a while, in the UK only.

By this time more money was coming into the Trust. Any gifts that are given to me for ministry are put into the Trust, and there are also a few regular contributors. I was working with various groups, but there was always a sense that I didn't belong anywhere. Yes, I was part of a church, but I wasn't part of a denomination or network. I felt I needed to be part of something. I wanted to be more accountable.

It was during my first trip to India with Ernest that I felt God was leading me to be part of the Assemblies of God (AoG) in the UK. It was something I had been thinking about, but while I was there I was able to ask Ernest about how I would go about joining the movement. He had been a minister with the AoG for many years.

The week after I got back from India in 2002, I had a meeting with an influential Christian leader named David Shearman. He is on my Council of Reference and is also one of the national leaders of the AoG. When I told him what I was thinking, he said, 'Everybody needs to belong somewhere.' He thought it would be a good move to associate with the AoG. So that was it for me; I took his advice to heart and began to make that happen.

I met up with my pastor, Alan Reeve, and told him that I believed that God was leading me to be part of the Assemblies of God. And he was fine with this, even though it meant that I was going to have to leave his church. He knew that it was time for me to move on.

Meanwhile I had arranged to have a meeting with Ian Watson, who is the senior leader of the Bridge Church in Bolton, which is a large AoG church. He agreed that I could base myself in his church and work out of there. I started the application process for ministerial status and then, in 2005, I completed my training and was ordained a minister with the Assemblies of God. This means that they recognize my gifting as an evangelist.

Also in 2005 I was invited to become an associate of one of the leading evangelistic communicators in the UK – J.John. I had first made a connection with him when I was a student at Cliff College; then later our paths crossed again. One thing led to another, and eventually he invited me to join his group of associate evangelists. His advice and help has proved to be invaluable to the life of the Trust.

At the beginning of 2006 we moved Proclaim Trust out of Champness Hall and into some new offices. This gave us the extra room that we needed to accommodate the staff and the growing ministry. Over the years, as this work has grown and developed, we have seen more and more examples of God's power at work, convicting people and bringing them to faith, and also in the area of supernatural healings. There has also been a strong sense that God has been busy putting everything in place for whatever he has in store for the coming years. I am looking forward to playing my part in seeing God make a difference, first in the UK and then across the world.

Chapter 17

New Horizons

When I became a Christian I made the decision to avoid getting into another relationship. I'd left Tania about eleven years ago, and just a few months after that I'd had the disastrous one-night stand that had caused me so much unnecessary worry.

Now I wanted to be totally focused on what God had called me to do, and I didn't want any distractions. I did have some female friends, but that's all they were – just friends. It never occurred to me that things were about to change – but of course, they did.

In the year 2000 I was invited to a leaders' seminar at Champness Hall in Rochdale, where the Trust offices were based. This was a presentation about a new social action programme that was going to be starting in the area. The woman taking the seminar was called Tina and she was part of the leadership of a Christian youth work organization. She was setting up a social action department within this, called TouchBase. She was also one of the trainers for this organization and their Pastoral Officer; this meant that she would visit the teams based throughout the UK, doing training in Christian ministry and addressing any issues that had arisen.

I could tell from her accent that she was from the South. She was an attractive woman: slim with blonde hair, and I guessed she was in her late twenties. I could see that she was passionate about God and the work she was involved with.

A few months after the seminar, Tina moved into the area and began to get the new venture off the ground. She was given some offices to work from in Champness Hall, so we were both based in the same building. Occasionally our paths would cross and we would have brief conversations, but that was it. I wasn't interested in anything more than that, and neither was she.

One afternoon the owner of Champness Hall, David, invited me to a barbeque. My flat was next to his house, so the event was effectively in my back garden. I came out for this barbeque and then Tina arrived; he had invited her as well. That afternoon she and I got the chance to chat together. She asked me if I had any hobbies.

'Well, I like to read,' I said, 'and I also quite like going to the cinema. What about you?'

'That's the kind of thing I like doing,' she said, and so we discovered that we had similar interests.

Life continued, and we would bump into each other at work from time to time, but that was about it. Tina was busy with her work and I was busy with mine. Then, just before Champness Hall closed for the Christmas holidays in 2002, I saw her in the central office when I was picking mail up.

'Hi, Tina,' I said. 'How you doing?'

'I'm fine; you working hard, then?'

'Yes, as always. You're staying in Rochdale over Christmas, aren't you?' I asked.

'Yes, I am,' she replied.

'Do you want to go out for a meal sometime over the holidays?'

She said yes, and so we made plans to go out for dinner.

When I was at college I would occasionally go out with a girl for a meal, and we would go just as friends. I even had one or two female friends in Rochdale whom I would sometimes go out with. These were completely platonic relationships and I was absolutely clear in my mind that the situation was not going to change.

Tina and I went out to a restaurant called Frankie and Benny's one afternoon; we had a meal and talked about God and the ministry that we were both involved with. It was a very enjoyable time; she was intelligent and she was full on for God. I liked spending time with her, but again, I didn't think too much more about it.

After the Christmas holidays had finished, we were both back in our respective offices and, from time to time, I would pop in to see how she was and have a chat. This went on for about a year. We could go for weeks without bumping into each other. I would be travelling across the UK and even to different parts of the world, and she would be on the road doing her visits to the teams and running TouchBase. She was also in the process of setting up a USA-based youth work team for the Christian organization she worked for, so she was spending quite a bit of time over there getting things off the ground. We were like ships in the night, passing occasionally – but that was fine, because we were also two adults who loved God and who had no intentions of having a relationship.

Then, one day in early 2003, I saw that she was in her office, so I popped in to see her.

'How's it going, then, Tina?'

'Fine thanks; I'm a bit busy at the moment. How about you – what are you up to?'

'Well I've been quite busy too. I've just got back from a mission in Argentina, but I'm going to be in the UK for a while now. Do you fancy going out for another meal sometime?

'Yes,' she said, 'that would be good.'

So I picked her up later and we went out for the evening. We had a good chat and an enjoyable time. When I dropped her off, I suggested that we do it again, and she said okay. Then about a month passed, and we went out again. We had a great night; all she talked about was God.

One of the things that I was sure about was that if I was ever to 'settle down', the woman I was with would have to be totally sold out for God – and Tina is definitely sold out for God!

A few weeks after this, we went out again. We were in an Indian restaurant near Rochdale. I was sat opposite her, and while we were chatting I suddenly thought, *Doesn't she smell nice! Isn't she sexy!*

She got up to go to the bathroom, and I looked and I thought, *Wow, she's beautiful! Look at her curves!*

I caught myself thinking these things, and I said to myself, *I can't think like this. It's wrong – we're just friends. There's nothing in it!*

I dropped her back home and then, when I got back into my flat, I felt really guilty. I hadn't looked at women in that way for years – I found her really attractive! The perfume that she had worn had smelt really feminine. I sat on my settee and started to talk to God, asking his forgiveness for thinking such things. After all, we were just friends, right?

Now, I have always found members of the opposite sex attractive. That's normal. It's part of a male's DNA. But this was something a bit more than that.

The next day I saw her walking through the corridor at work, and I thought, *I really am starting to fancy her.*

I tried to shrug this off, but it wouldn't leave me. Then it dawned on me that this could be a God thing. I had said that I wanted to stay single so I could just get on with ministry, and for years I had done just that. But now the way that I was thinking was changing. I was thinking about how I could still do the work if I was married, and how my wife and I could complement each other. This type of thinking was new to me.

Soon after this, we went out again. I picked her up from her flat, and when she walked out of the door she looked gorgeous. I could tell she had made an effort to look good, and I started to ask myself, *Does she like me?*

I began to think about this more and more, and then one night I decided to send her an email. I sat there on the settee in my flat with my laptop in front of me, and I didn't know where to start. For once, I was stuck for words. I wanted to get this right. I didn't want to sound too forward, I didn't want to ruin the friendship that we had, and I didn't know what she was thinking. I didn't know whether she wanted to be just friends or whether she wanted something more. Was she looking to settle down? These were the thoughts that were going through my mind when I was sat there. After about an hour I managed to compose a two-sentence email. It went something like this:

> Dear Tina
> Do you think that God could be in this relationship?
>   Look forward to hearing from you.
>   Barry

I sat there, waiting with anticipation. This was the first girl I had asked out since I had split up with Tania in 1992. I had a feeling in my stomach; what if she says no? What would I do then? It was like being 16 again!

After five minutes I received an email back from her. I opened it quickly, and it said:

Dear Barry
I like to think that God is in all of our relationships.
  Thanks

Tina

And I thought: *Oh no! I know that God is in all our relationships, but that's not what I meant. Surely she knows what I'm trying to say.*

This was all so new; in the old days I'd have been straight in there. This was not my first relationship but it was my first romance. It really brought home to me the concept of being a new person in Christ.

I replied to her email, and this is what I wrote:

Dear Tina
I know that God is in all our relationships, but do you think he has brought us together for a purpose?
Barry

Within minutes she emailed back and said 'Yes, maybe.' That's all she said. She wasn't making this easy for me, but I could see that she was interested. Tina had been single for seven years and she just wanted to be careful, like I was being careful.

Later that week, I took her for another meal. But this time it was different because we were going out on a date. It was great! After all the stuff I had been through in the past, here I was, going out with this great woman. It felt quite strange because this dating thing was new to me. I had had all this life experience, but I felt that I was doing this for the first time. I felt like God had brought us together. Over the next few months we continued to go out.

Meanwhile, I had developed a great relationship with my parents again – the best it had ever been. Since I had become a Christian they had both seen the huge change in me; and as the years went by, they began to see that this wasn't a passing fad, or another drug-induced fantasy; they could see that my faith was real. They had started to trust me again. I realized what fantastic parents they had been and I started to appreciate them more and more. I would go out of my way to call them, wherever I was in the world; I would phone them on a regular basis. If I was at home, I visited them as often as I could.

Any time my dad asked me about girls, I would say I wasn't interested, because I wanted to be free to get on with the work that God had called me to. My dad isn't a Christian so he didn't understand. After all, isn't it normal for a young guy like me to have a girlfriend? I think sometimes he may have been a bit worried that I had lost interest in girls, because I had been single for so long. He knew that I hadn't really, but he was a bit suspicious. I hadn't had a girlfriend for nearly eleven years.

After Tina and I had started to date, I told my mam and dad that I had a girlfriend. They were both over the moon – especially my dad! I told them all about her – where she was from and what she did. They were well chuffed! So after a few weeks I took Tina to meet them. It was a big deal for us, and I think it was for them too.

My mam was sat in her chair in one corner of the room and my dad was sat in his chair near the window. Tina followed me into the living-room and then I said, 'Mam, Dad – this is Tina, the girl I told you about.'

My mam had a smile on her face, and said, 'Pleased to meet you, Tina.'

And then my Dad said, 'How you doin', love? Sit down.'

So my mam and dad got to meet Tina, and they were both really chuffed. The 'meet the parents' bit went as well as it possibly could.

Over the next month Tina and I got to know each other, and by this time we were both sure that this was a God thing – that God was in the relationship and that he had brought us together. After giving it some thought, I asked her if she would marry me. In the past I'd had long-term relationships, but I had never got married. Maybe God had something to do with this; maybe he knew that one day I was going to make a connection with him, and he had Tina lined up for me.

I was thrilled when she accepted my proposal, and a few days after this we went to see my mam and dad again to tell them the news.

'Dad,' I said, 'I've got something to tell you.'

'What is it?' said my dad, and he turned the TV off. Now, in my mam and dad's house the TV is always on in the evenings, so for him to turn it off was a significant thing.

'Well, Tina and I are getting engaged. We're going to get married next year.'

'Is that right?' said my dad. 'Well I never ...'

I looked at my mam, and she had a little tear in her eye. All she had wanted for me since I had left school was that I should find a good woman and settle down and get married.

We were married on 7 February 2004. We invited just family and close friends and had a small wedding ceremony at the Kingsway Church in Wombourne in the Midlands.

We had our honeymoon in Cuba and then, after getting back, we moved into a small terraced house that we had bought just before the wedding, and we started our life together.

By the time we were married Tina had left the youth work organization she had been working for, and later she started to work for Proclaim Trust part time.

Before we moved into our new offices in 2006 we decorated all the way through, then we moved in all the
furniture and added some extra things. In my office
there is a large wall and I said to Tina that I wanted to
put something really significant on that wall. Three
weeks after we had moved in, I was having a look
around an art shop, and I came across a painting called
New Horizons. It shows a beautiful horizon across a
wide expanse. I saw this and thought: *That's it. That's
what needs to go on my wall.*

I took it back to the office. I put it on the wall, and
every day when I'm in the office, I can look up at the picture and be reminded that God is a God of New
Horizons! Since the day when I walked into that church
and had that encounter with God, there has been one
new horizon after another. Some of them I could see
coming, like getting an education or working as an
evangelist or even travelling to various parts of the
world; but some have taken me completely by surprise,
like meeting Tina. I know that God has been with me all
the way through all of the things that have happened to
me. It's been an amazing journey, and it hasn't finished
yet. I have a strong sense that there are many more new
horizons to come!

I want to draw to a close now by saying a few words
to you, the reader.

This book has been an honest account of my life. You
have read about how I was totally transformed by the
power of God, and how God has painted a number of
new horizons for my life. He can do the same for you!
And the new horizons he has for you may be different
from the ones he has for me. You could be living the kind
of life that I once lived or your life may be completely
different. In fact, your life could be totally opposite to
mine. I always say there are two types of people who are

part of the Christian church. There are those who can talk about what God has saved them from – that's a person like me – and we are the minority. Then there are those who can talk about what God has kept them from – that's those who have lived respectable lives – they are the majority. It doesn't matter which kind you are, because the Christian message is for everybody. That means you!

Let me explain. The Bible is an instruction book. The letters B.I.B.L.E stand for Basic Instructions Before Leaving Earth. The Bible teaches us that we have all sinned (bad thoughts, bad words and bad actions) and fallen short of God's standards. I know that you know that you are not perfect. None of us are; we have all made mistakes, we have all sinned. But the Bible tells us that God is perfect and holy, and that the sin that is in our lives separates us from him. It teaches us that sin creates a barrier between us and God, and that God's remedy for this was to send his Son Jesus Christ into the world to die on the cross to pay the penalty for that sin. The Bible also explains that if we turn from our sin and put our trust in his Son Jesus and receive him into our life, he will forgive us for our past and give us a brand-new start; to put it another way, he will paint a new horizon for us! This is the first of many.

You may be reading this and thinking to yourself: *I want God to paint this new horizon for me, but I don't know what to do.* Well, I can help you: this is what you need to do. First, you need to accept that you have sinned and you have made mistakes. Secondly, you need to believe that Jesus Christ died on the cross and that he rose again. Thirdly, you need to commit you life to God. That's what you need to do. When you do these three things, God will then get out his paintbrush and start to paint a whole new future for you!

You could be reading this book, and you are a Christian and you have been challenged about your lifestyle and your commitment to Christ. You know that you are not living the life that God wants you to live. Listen: you need to get back on track by making a re-commitment to Christ so that God can paint another new horizon for you!

I'm going to finish this book by leading you, the reader, in a simple prayer. This is the same prayer that I prayed at that rail in Dearnley Methodist Church in 1995. This prayer will start you on your journey with God. If you want to receive Christ into your life for the first time, or if you want to re-commit your life so that you can get back on track, please pray this prayer out loud:

> Dear Lord Jesus, I come to you today and I confess that I need you. Please come into my heart. Jesus, be my Lord and Saviour. Thank you for giving me a brand-new start. Wash me, cleanse me and forgive all my sins. Today I open my life to you. I know I am a child of the king.

Now you have prayed that prayer, you need to do these three things so that you can move on in your journey and grow.

First, you need to get a Bible. This is what I did when I had made a decision to receive Christ into my life. Remember, I said in this book that one of the first things I did was start reading the Bible. I couldn't get enough of it.

The Bible is not one book that's to be read from front to back like you would usually read a book. It's actually sixty-six small books within one cover. It comes in two parts – Part 1 and Part 2 – or, the Old Testament and the New Testament. Start by reading the book of John in the

New Testament. You don't have to spend eight hours a day reading it like I did; just start by reading two chapters a day. You could also find a Christian bookstore nearby and ask them for some material to help you read your Bible. You will find that as you read it, God will speak to you, just like he does with me.

Another thing you need to do is to start to pray. I discovered early on in my journey that this was one of the best things I can do. Prayer is basically talking to God. When we make a decision to receive Christ into our life, God becomes our Father, and he wants us to talk to him. You don't have to use big and fancy words when you pray; just be real and chat to God, but remember who you are talking to! More than anything, God wants us to have a one-to-one with him. He want's to be involved with our life. When we pray, that's what we are doing.

The third thing you need to do is to find a Christian church. That's what I did. God doesn't want us to go it alone. He wants us to make friends and come together to spend time worshipping him. That's why there are churches around. Don't just go to any church; it's important that you find one where the people believe that the Bible is true, and where Jesus is central to their teaching. It was during my time at the Branches Church that I grew in my faith. There were people in the church who were there to help me if I needed it. You may even know someone who goes to church. Ask them to take you with them and ask them to introduce you to the minister.

You could also look at this website: www.christianity.org.uk. This provides basic information on all the major churches in the UK and Ireland.

Thank you for taking the time to read this book. I hope that, as you have been reading it, you have been inspired and challenged. But most of all, I hope that you have seen that God can truly work in the life of an individual. I know this is true, because I was once an addict, and now I'm clean.

Proclaim Trust

If you would like more information about the ministry of Proclaim Trust, please go to our website:
www.proclaimtrust.org

If you would like to book Barry to speak at a mission, event or conference, then please email:
info@proclaimtrust.org

Alternatively, you can contact us at:

Proclaim Trust
PO Box 550
Rochdale
Greater Manchester
OL16 9EJ
United Kingdom

Telephone/Fax: +44 (0) 1706 638803